TEN HOUSES

TEN HOUSES

Edited by Oscar Riera Ojeda

Christian De Groote

First published in the United States of America by:
Rockport Publishers Inc.
33 Commercial Street
Gloucester, Massachusetts 01930
Telephone: 978-282-9590
Fax: 978-283-2742

Distributed to the book trade and art trade in the United States of America by
North Light Books, an imprint of F & W Publications
1504 Dana Avenue
Cincinnati, Ohio 45207
Telephone: 513-531-2222

Other distribution by
Rockport Publishers Inc.

ISBN 1-56496-492-2
10 9 8 7 6 5 4 3 2 1

Printed in China

Cover Photograph: The "El Condor" Group. Photograph by Luis Poirot
Back Cover Photographs are of projects on pages (from left, top to bottom) 18, 28, 38, 46, 56, 76, 64, 84, 92, 102
Page 2: The "El Condor" Group. Photograph by Luis Poirot

Graphic Design: Lucas H. Guerra / Oscar Riera Ojeda
Layout: Oscar Riera Ojeda
Composition: Hunha Lee

Contents

Selected Works

Such gestures challenge the so-called "regionalist architectures" that seek to reconcile building and context by means of vernacular idioms, traditional materials, and modes of construction. De Groote recognizes the radical artifice in architecture. He has no use for organic camouflage to converse with the natural and built environments. His insubordination to the authority of tradition and context allows him to tailor his designs to the dweller's desire in both symbolic and pragmatic matters of inhabitation. Each house has a distinct flavor and a particular principle of organization. It is precisely tuned to the functional aspects of everyday life but also invested in meaningful representations of dwelling. The house is a faithful portrait, so to speak, of a unique lifestyle.

Continuing with the painterly analogy, we may think of de Groote's domestic architecture as a synthesis of the landscape and portrait genres. The hybrid is neither smooth nor always happy. Nevertheless, it yields consistently compelling demonstrations showing that civic and environmental responsibility do not preclude the affirmation of character and individuality.

Ross House (above), Pedro Pablo Errazuriz (right), both in Santiago, Chile

Rodolphe el-Khoury *is an architect, critic, and historian who teaches at the Harvard Graduate School of Design.*

Introduction

by Christian de Groote

On speaking of my firm's work—represented by the ten houses displayed in detail in this book—it's important to stress a fundamental characteristic common to all of them: each was conceived for a specific client.

In these times, more and more distance separates the user and the architect. To combat this syndrome, our firm stubbornly upholds a mandatory rule before accepting a commission to build a house: the client must be, at the same time, the user of the house. I simply cannot approach a project leaning exclusively on my own subjectivity, or as a pure exercise of personal interests. Without that gravity center—the "form-user" relation—the architecture would lose the anchor that protects it against spurious influences such as fashion, ideologies, and trends, leaving it bare of the basic consistency I intend to achieve.

This has led me to persistently avoid merely speculative architecture, the kind requested by a client on behalf of a third party, the most common basis of the professional practice not only in Chile, but everywhere. Abstract speculation is not my working method. The works do not stem from a theoretical stance, or from the adherence to a specific school or movement. Behind them there is neither a supporting philosophy nor an intellectual scaffolding to give them a validity beyond the precise and concrete results represented by the work itself.

There is, indeed, a working method lending my architecture a disciplinary context through the persistence of a set of habits and procedures to face different problems. I do not have a stance prior to any specific project, but the feeling of starting a journey down a well-known path. At this point, the journey has acquired characteristics of its own that are, up to a point, definable.

My approach to each work is never a priori, but is derivative from multiple elements coming from different spheres. That is why there is no stand previous

Left: *Slachevsky House, Santiago de Chile. This house, economically built in 1972, makes the most of its concrete-block construction, small size, and expressive set of volumes (derived from an inner ramp connecting the different levels).*

Opposite Page: *Lota House, Santiago de Chile. The influence of Le Corbusier on the architect's work is distinctly present in the design of this, his first house.*

to the work, nor an adherence to any trend or movement. Thus, there are no representational, stylistic or metaphorical concessions. "Not having a stance" is paramount to me; as an architect I consider myself an interpreter, and in order to be coherent with this role, one must face the works with the greatest possible bareness and spontaneity, literally, to turn oneself into a blank sheet.

Speaking specifically of the individual houses, I would like to stress something that I call, for lack of a better term, "the house as portrait of a family." This principle views the architect as translator, a person who, with greater or lesser sensibility, gathers every piece of information from the outside. Simply arranging them in a harmonious and disciplined manner, the architect does not betray this process. Thus, the architect creates a universe inspired not by his own inner world —indispensable though it is for him so as to properly process the information— but by the stimuli coming from outward sources, stimuli which must be interpreted with sensibility.

In this creative process, the client—understanding as such the individual, the couple, or the family—plays an essential role, being as he is the real protagonist of his own work, its veritable architect. In fact, most clients say they think of themselves as frustrated architects. This, which can be considered as a mere stock phrase, springs from the fact that to build is a fundamental human need that has very much to do with lasting and belonging. Architecture is closely related to culture and ritual, and obviously these aspects stem directly from the client, not from the architect.

In order to make the clients' stamp even more decisive, I always encourage them to actively participate during the building stage. I foster their stimulating collaboration and point them out how in every stage we are facing a living

material, generous to changes and adjustments. The excitement that they and I feel at being open to a world of surprises and possibilities creates affectionate, fruitful ties.

In that thing which is confession, psychoanalysis, subliminal data, bareness, the client transmits his own interests, habits, and longings, constructing his sphere of life in a vertical (instantaneous) and horizontal (in time) section. In the course of such rich and lively participation, the client takes over the leading part of the architectural process. Along these lines, this paragraph from Octavio Paz bears much significance:

From the moment I opened my eyes I realized that my place was not here, where I am now, but where I am not and never have been. There is an empty place somewhere, and that emptiness shall be full of me until I become a spring or a fountain. And my emptiness, that void of myself that I am now, will become filled up with itself, full of being to the brims.

I always endeavor to make my work contextual; my idea of context cannot be reduced either to the geographic issue or to the concept of place, exclusively. Context is for me something like the constellation of data surrounding the problem. Permanently on the alert, the architect constructively captures and interprets this data, which suggests ways of solution.

***Left: First Column Top and Center:** Calderón House, Santiago de Chile. The set of planes account for the rich inner spaces. First Column **Bottom:** Alcalde House, Santiago de Chile. One steady feature of the architect's residential work is the secluded nature of his houses. **Second Column Top and Center:** El Murciélago House, Santiago de Chile. The special volumetric characteristics of the three-story house dramatize the cordilleran landscape. **Second Column Bottom:** Pedro Pablo Errazuriz House, Santiago de Chile. The access pavement in stripes emphasizes the strong presence of the wall toward the street. **Third Column Top and Center:** Bernardo Matte House, Santiago de Chile. The richness of the access volumes and the large, double-height, inner loggia pay tribute to the magnificent cordilleran landscape. **Third Column Bottom:** Patricio de Groote House, Santiago de Chile. Its strong and simple volume is outlined against an impressive backdrop of hills.*
***Right:** Gora House, Zapallar, Chile. The fortress-like character of this work, entirely covered with local stone, corresponds to its outstanding location over a Pacific reef.*

The project introduces itself as a question, and is conceived through a long chain of deductions and experiences. The proposal stemming from this method is always radical, in the sense of being characteristic and exclusive of that particular work. It's also basic, in the sense of being simple but strong. It is the imperative result of the conditions granting the work a life of its own, conditions which exclude any conception of architecture as something autonomous, as opposed to the other arts in general.

Just as it is obvious that with regard to industrial buildings the imperatives of the process weigh down heavily on the design, it is evident to me, or at least to my way of working, that in a more subtle and concealed manner, indeed much more difficult to grasp, the work of architecture is fundamentally determined from the outside.

Le Corbusier said to architecture students: "The teachers who look after your instruction should only open for you the doors to expanses irremediably free of limits. The diploma crowning your studies should bestow a single right: that of overstepping the threshold." Well, I have spent all my life as an architect in pursuit of the opposite, in search of limits, the more precise the better, since that freedom Le Corbusier speaks of is only at the disposal of the chosen.

The role I ascribe to the client may seem surprising in view of the absence of conventionalism and the apparent formal disparity of the houses I have made, which seem unilaterally generated by the mere will of the architect. Still, I have three plain evidences to sustain what I say:

- First, my professional experience has invariably demonstrated that there is a direct relationship between the result of the work, in terms of its architectural quality, the "client's" sensibility, and the depth of his involvement;
- Second, the inner experience of feeling totally alien to the work once it is finished; to remain aloof in order to look at it and appreciate it with the eyes of an architect, not an author; and

Left and Opposite Page: *FAT House, Santiago de Chile. The magnificent and lavish vegetation existing at the site entirely determined the architecture of this work.*

Third, the birth of a bond, of an unusual link with the client, which has a bit of complicity, shyness, a great deal of affection, and a certain uneasiness. The whole process is somewhat heartbreaking. One has left in the work a piece of oneself.

Barragán used to say that his architecture was autobiographic. I regard mine as biographic. I also wish to refer to a unique and singular aspect of these ten houses in particular, and of all my work in general, consisting in its relation with the geographical context in which they are inserted. I believe that American architecture has not been up to the challenge posed by our particular, varied and, at times, extraordinary geography; it has not been able to serve as a basis for a real counterpoint between man's work and his natural surrounding. This failure is especially evident when we compare our present architecture with that of the Aztecs, Mayas, or Incas.

Perhaps the sole and rare exceptions can be found in Mexico and, on a lesser scale, in Brazil. It is my goal to create an architecture in accordance with its geographic context and, furthermore, a geographical architecture—architecture as a geographical event.

The starting point of this reasoning is that nature is in a state of hibernation until the imprint of man appears, as if it were a motionless and silent film. A man's footprints on the sand suffice to turn that which is natural into an architectural event that withdraws geography from its connotation of pre-creation, as a river that does not exist while there is no bridge crossing it.

Many interpretations have been woven round the joy that the contemplation of ruins has produced in all people at all times, due to their beauty, their mystery and evocative power, and their propensity for making us feel immersed in the depths of time. My own interpretation is that this broken beauty, this disintegration, the crumbling, the disappearance of all that is superfluous and perishable, lend ruins that veritable and proper coupling with nature which my architecture seeks to reproduce.

This Page and Opposite Page: Paulina House, Santiago, Chile. The volumes are determined by the steep slope and the rich variety of native trees covering the site.

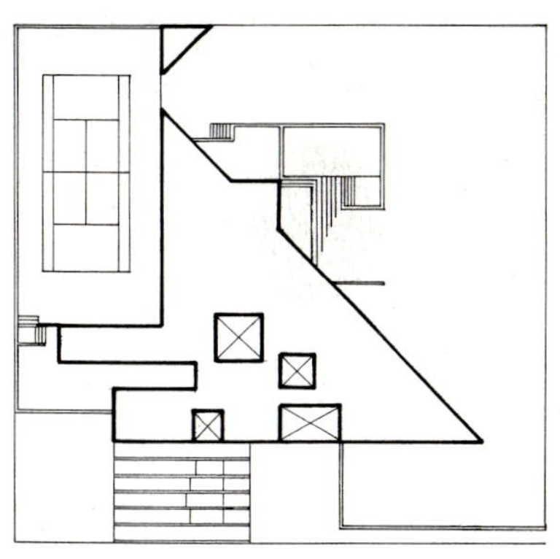

Site Plan

A

1. Entrance
2. Carport
3. Entrance Hall
4. Interior Garden
5. Studio
6. Living Room
7. Dining Room
8. Kitchen
9. Laundry
10. Service Room
11. Mechanical
12. Tennis Court
13. Pool
14. Terrace
15. Master Bedroom
16. Bedroom
17. Family Room
18. Dressing Room
19. Service Yard

Floor Plan

A

0   5   10   15   20m

Garcia House

Santiago, Chile

Located in Las Condes, this 43,000-square-foot (4,000-square-meter) site ended up rather small for developing this very ambitious program that included a tennis court that, by itself, required a fifth of the available area. At the client's request, the house included a study connected to the master bedroom that also faces an inner patio, giving the study total privacy. This requirement allowed us to make a quite dense ground plan.

As the axis of the view toward the Andes mountains follows a forty-five-degree deviation in relation to the site, we placed the tennis court close to a corner and the house against it, laying out the site on a large diagonal and forming two triangles. The house and the tennis court occupy one of these triangles, and the garden occupies the other. This produces the impression of an open area much larger than it really is, while giving the house a long front facing the mountains.

The dense and compact form established by the equilateral triangle becomes lighter with the creation of inner patios, which articulate the ground plan and define the different areas of the program. The exterior is treated with painted rough stucco, and the interior is completely lined with honey-colored raw silk paneling, lending the house unity and continuity. The only element that differs is the great exposed concrete beam crowning the diagonal of the house, emphasizing its large dimension.

Above: *Aerial view of the house, still under construction, showing how the inner patios shape an orthogonal plan without interfering with the large diagonal toward the garden.*

Opposite Page: *An orthogonal plane that enlarges the area of terraces near the swimming pool intercepts the long diagonal concrete beam.*

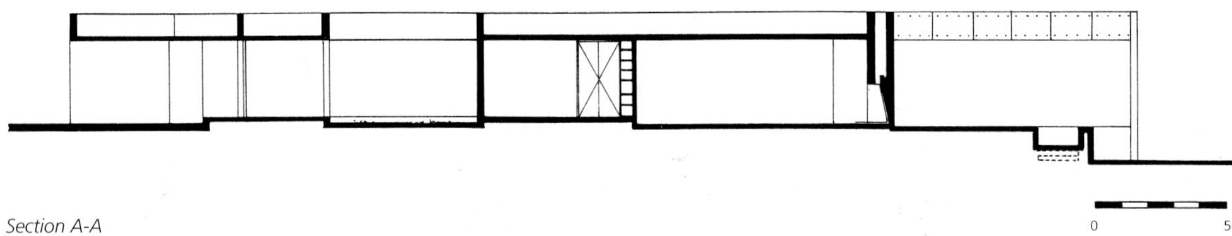

Section A-A

0   5m

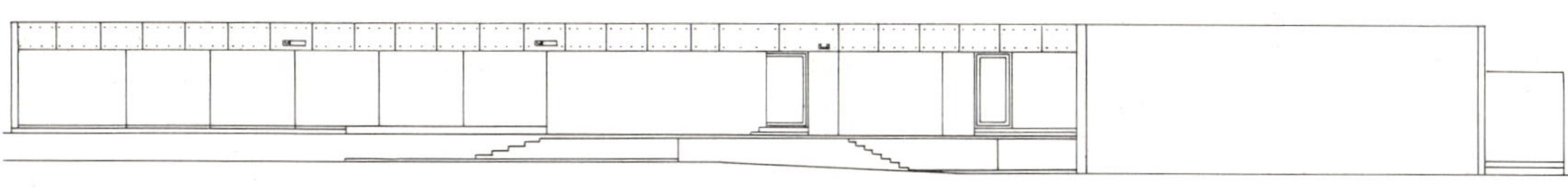

North Elevation

0   3m

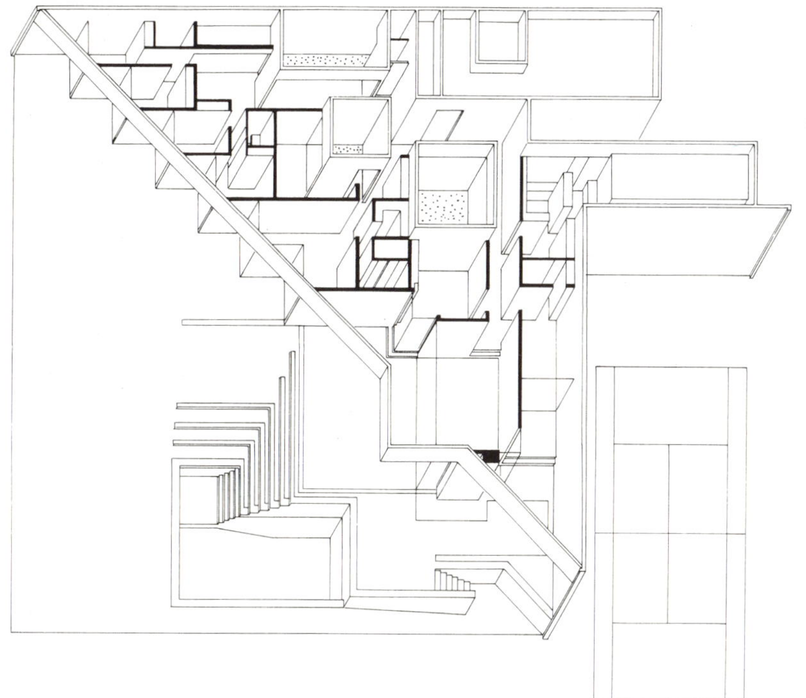

Axonometric View

Section B-B

0   5m

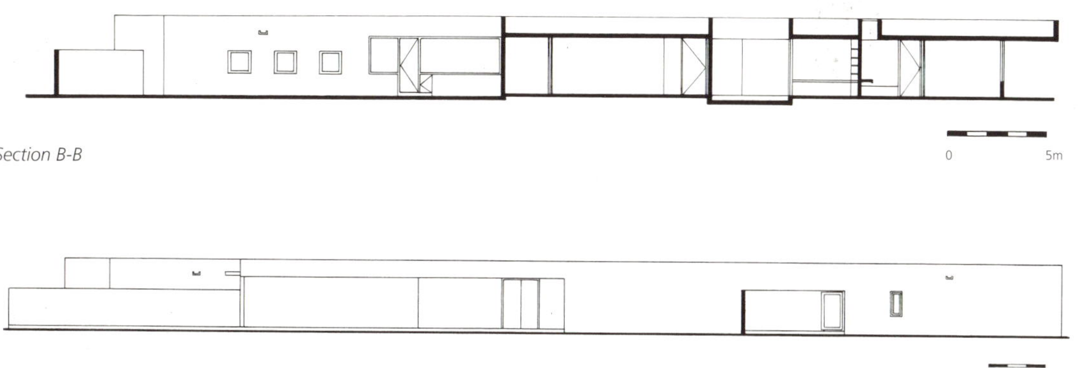

South Elevation

0   3m

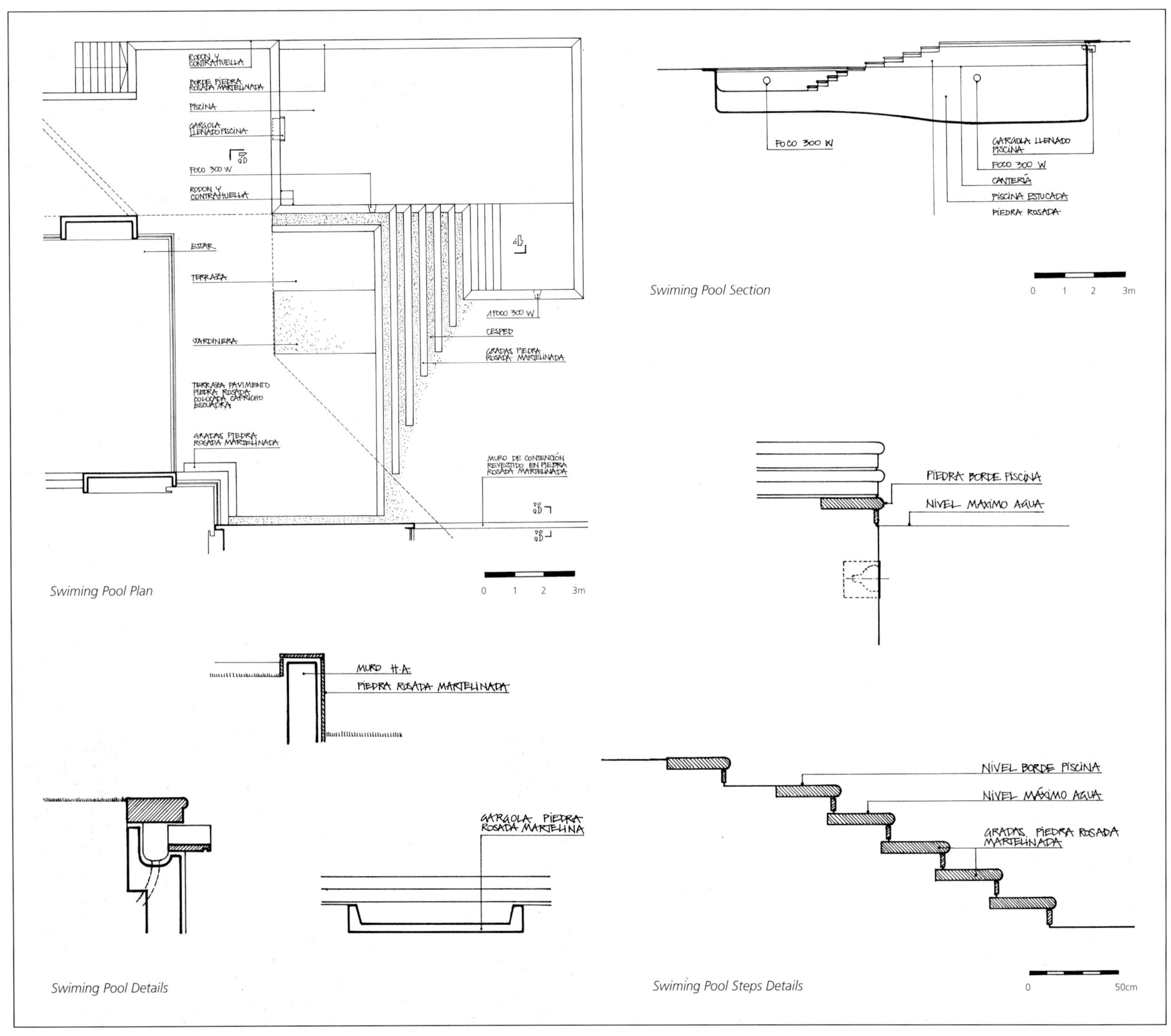

Swiming Pool Plan

Swiming Pool Section

Swiming Pool Details

Swiming Pool Steps Details

0 1 2 3m

0 1 2 3m

0 50cm

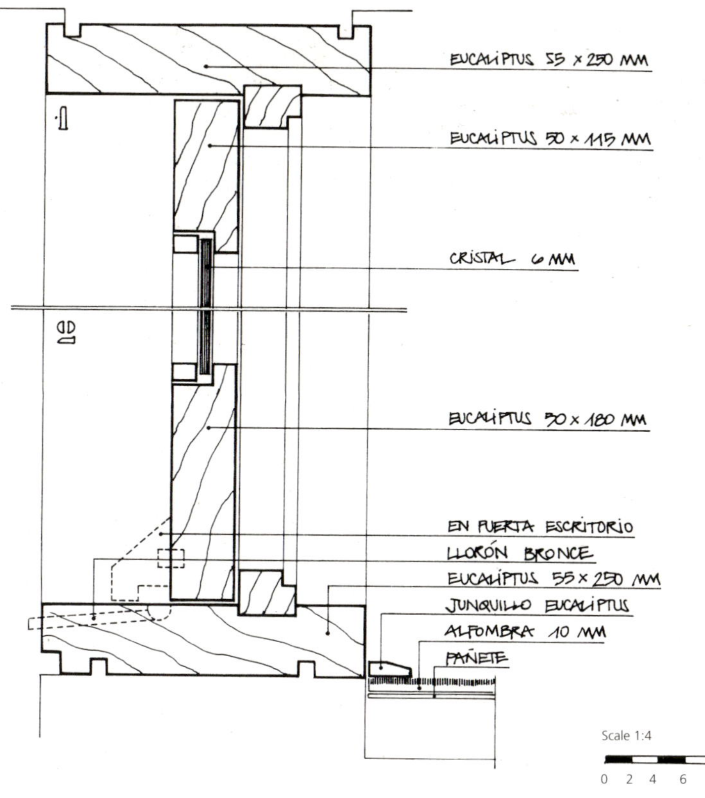

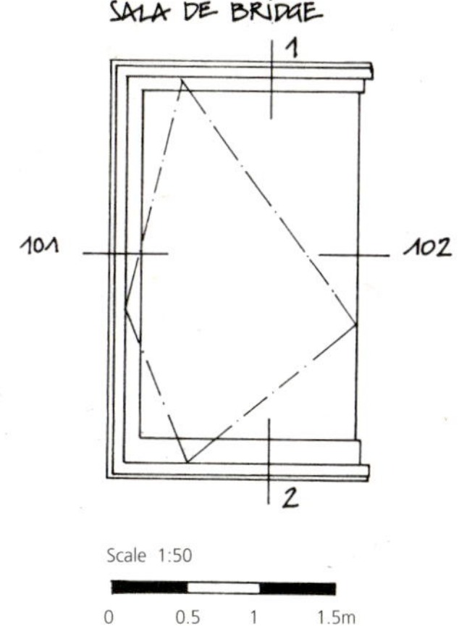

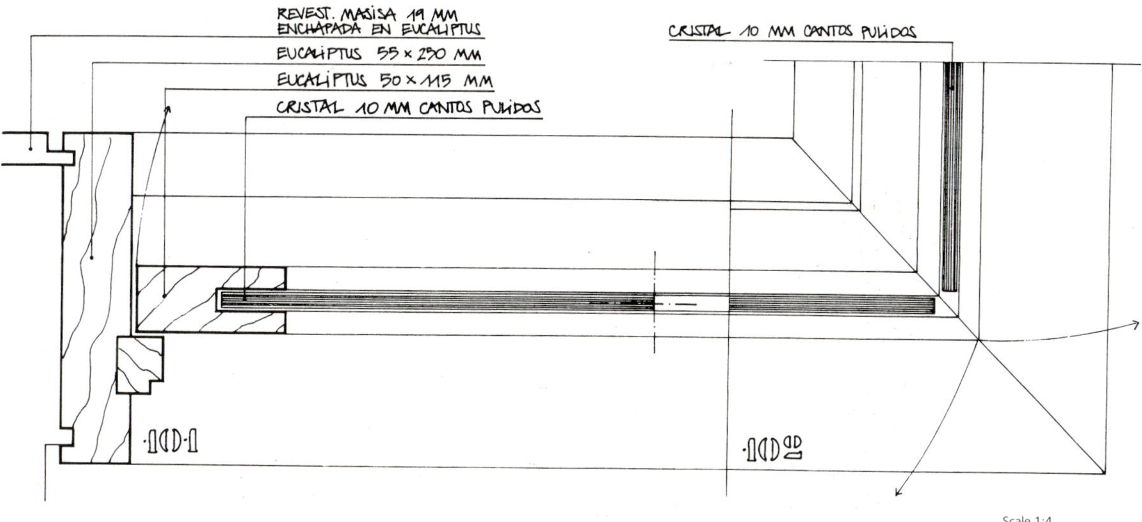

Wood Door/Window Details (Garden Elevation)

Constanza Vergara House

Algarrobo, Chile

A sea resort on the Pacific, Algarrobo lies approximately 75 miles (120 kilometers) to the southwest of Santiago. This house is located at the northern end of the town, Algarrobo's oldest and most urban area. The site, very small in size—approximately 4,750 square feet (440 square meters)—is set directly in front of the beach about seven feet (two meters) above the sand.

Conceived as a totally blind back, the street façade consists of a completely blank stone wall in keeping with the character of the neighboring houses. Developed on different planes, the façade produces a sort of bow that marks the beginning of the resort's urban area. The side facing the sea comprises wood and glass, somehow relating the house to the light and graceful architecture of the yachts that sail Algarrobo's small bay. This façade is broken with regard to the orthogonal system of the house structure, in order to face the living room toward the best view and to stress the idea of the house as the end of the urban complex.

Both inside and outside the house, white and black ceramic floor tiling resembles a chess board and enhances the feeling of leisure and ease. At the sight level of a person sitting inside the house or on the terrace, there is only sea to contemplate, such as when sailing. On the other hand, the view from the master bedroom on the second floor, with its large floor-to-ceiling windows, becomes dramatic with the to-and-fro of the waves. All the wood employed, both in the structure and in the covering, is Oregon pine with a honey varnish that lends the house a warm quality.

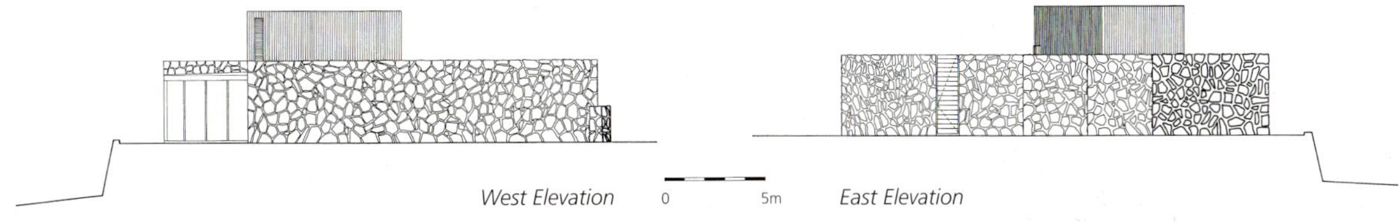

__Above:__ The volume in wood, corresponding to the master bedroom, shows over the stone wall toward the street. A beautiful tree acts as a natural canopy at the entrance.

__Opposite:__ The rhythm of the windows clearly registers the structure of the wooden posts and beams.

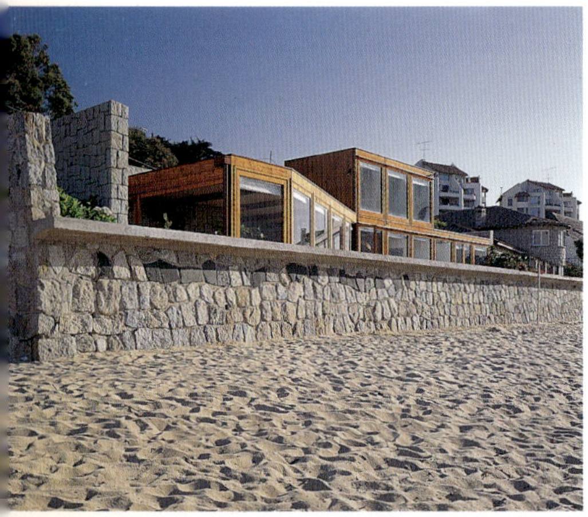

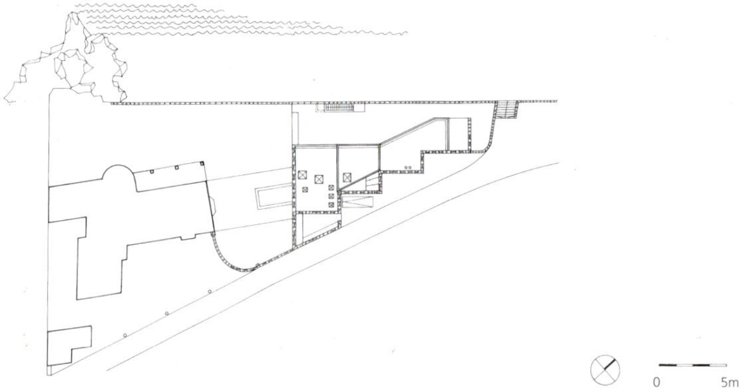

Site Plan

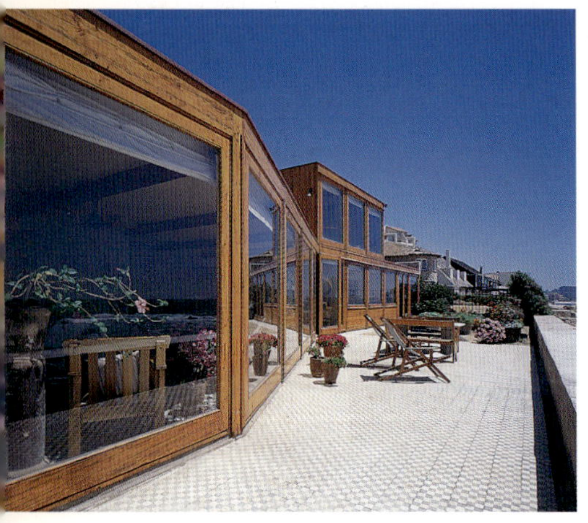

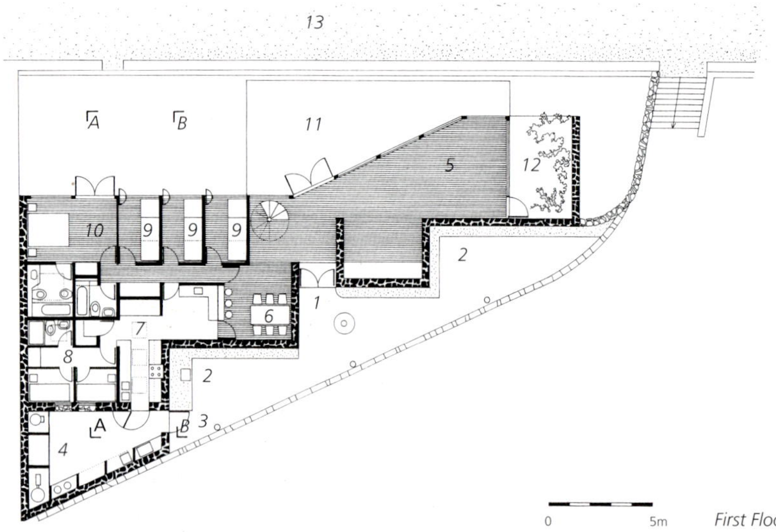

First Floor Plan

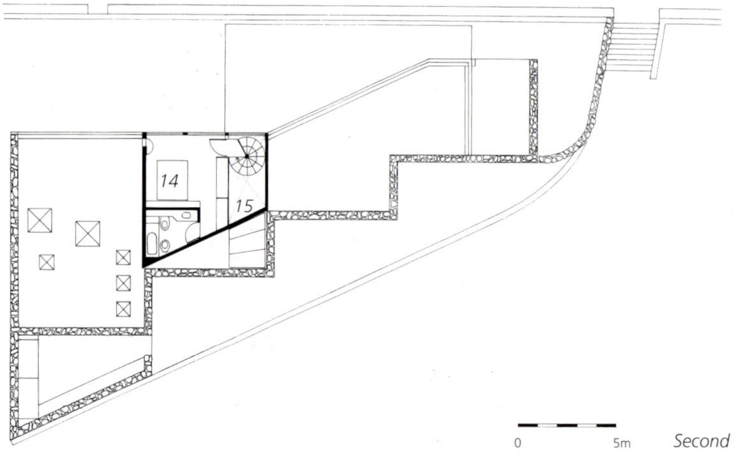

Second Floor Plan

1. Entrance
2. Parking
3. Service Entrance
4. Service Patio
5. Living Room
6. Dining Room
7. Kitchen
8. Service Bedroom
9. Children Bedroom
10. Guest Bedroom
11. Terrace
12. Garden Patio
13. Beach
14. Master Bedroom
15. Void

Opposite Page: *The spiral wooden staircase is inserted in the double-height space connecting the living room and the master bedroom.*

This Page: *The inner space opens uninterrupted toward the terrace and the sea; the stone railing also operates as a breakwater.*

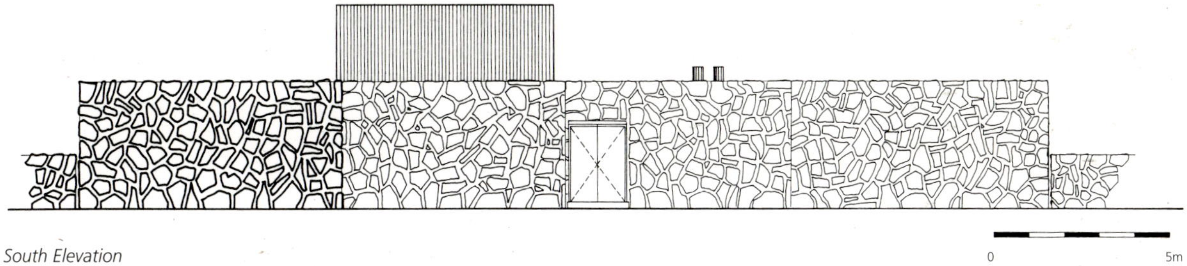

South Elevation

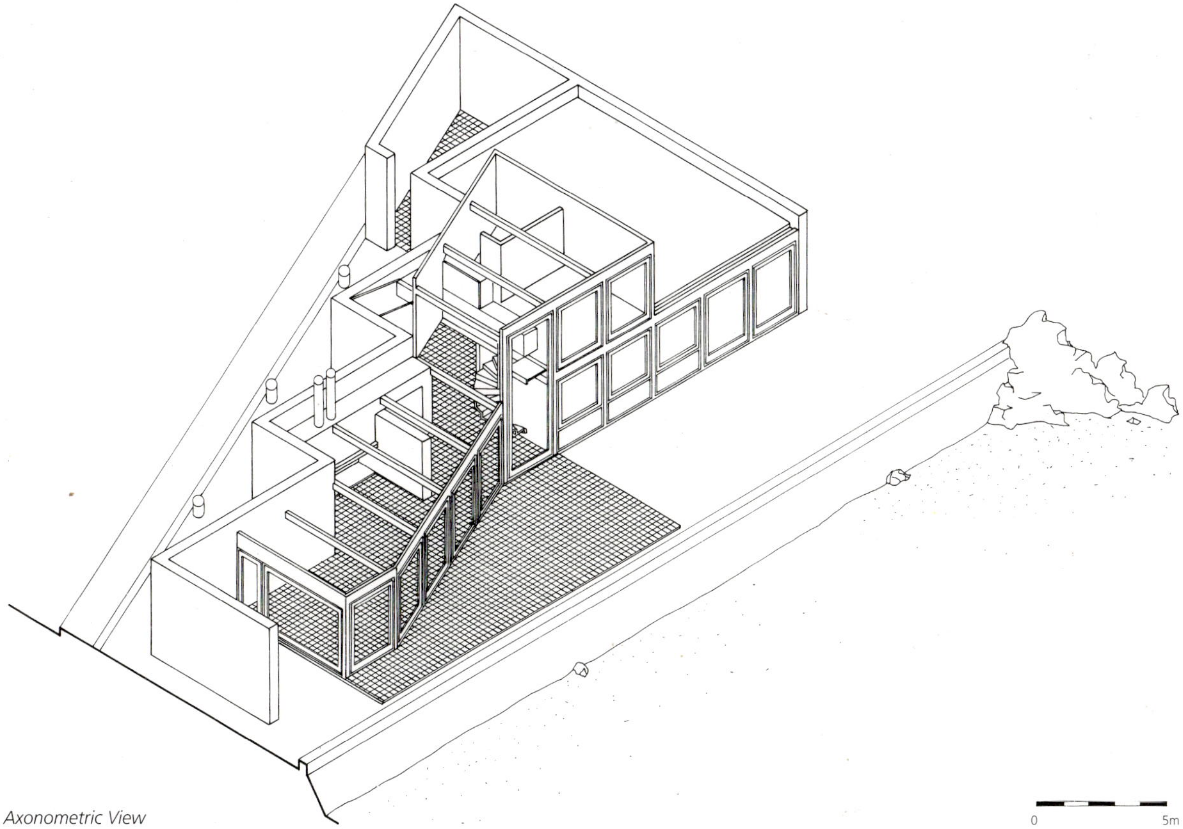

Axonometric View

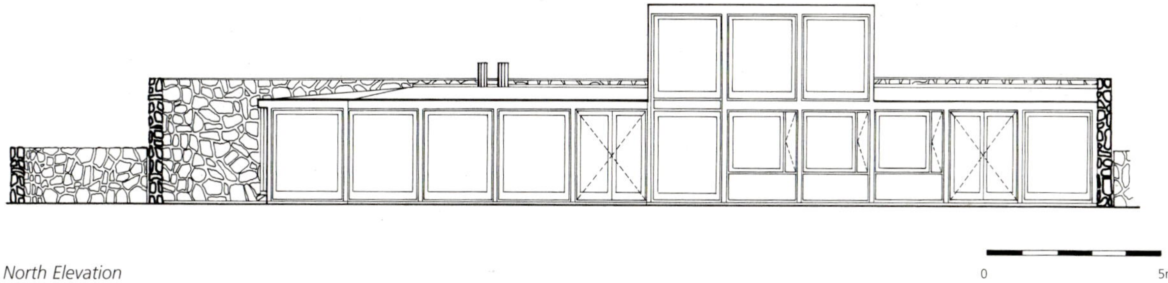

North Elevation

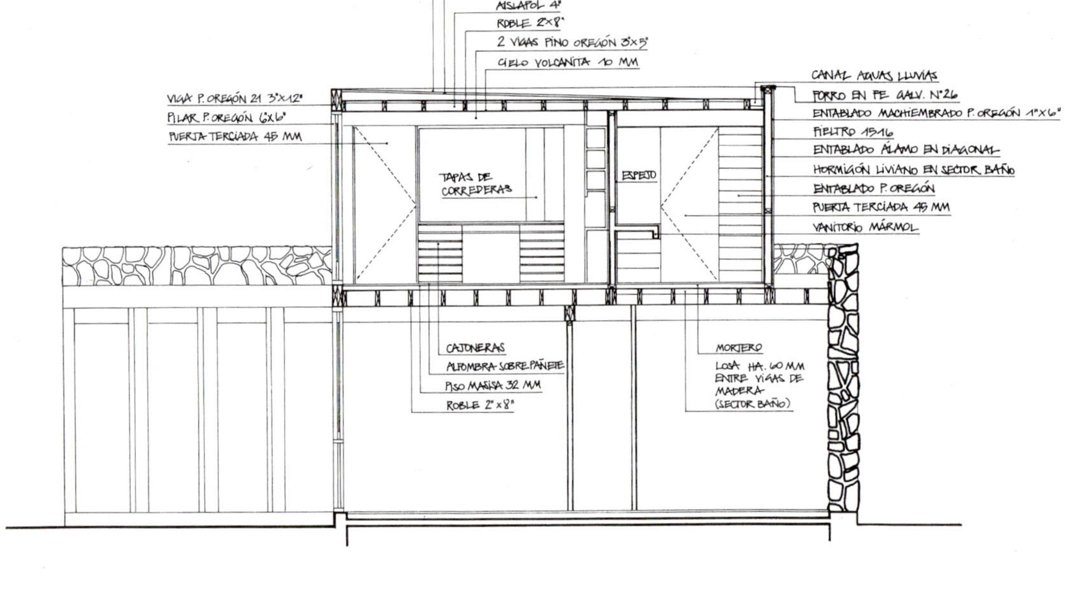

Section B-B

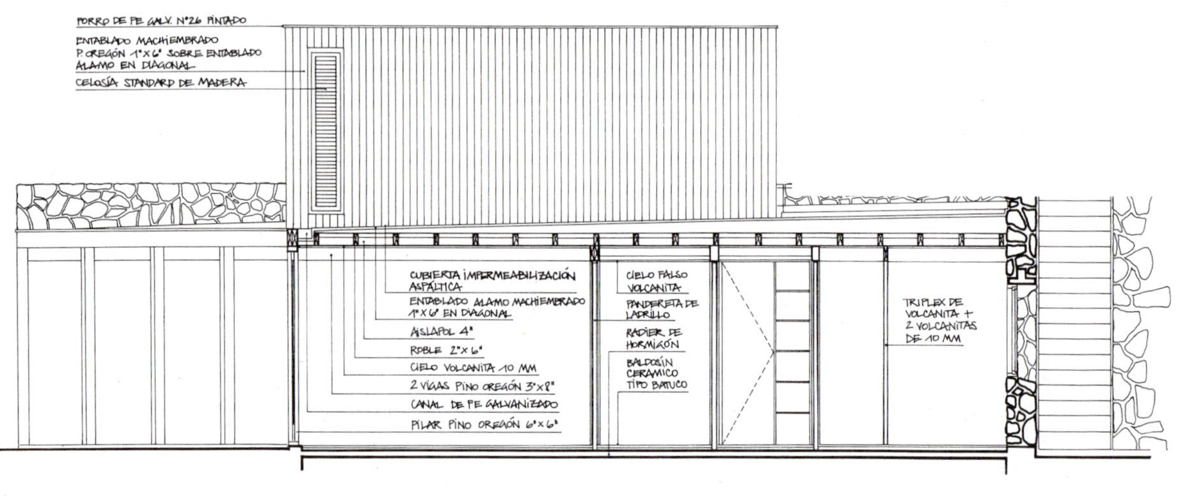

Section A-A

0   1   2m

Fuenzalida House

Santiago, Chile

The house is located in the northeastern quadrant of Santiago, in the beautiful mountain valley of La Dehesa. Long and narrow (112 by 230 feet/34 by 70 meters), the site contains a pronounced slope in the lengthwise, north-south direction, and a spectacular view of the mountains toward the east. The geography has such a strong presence—and at the time there were so few buildings in the valley—that it was only natural to opt for a bare, firm position that balances the landscape.

The house was conceived as a great horizontal volume almost 154 feet (47 meters) long by 26 feet (8 meters) wide, which acts as a sort of "mason's level" on a geographical scale, drawing a long horizontal line acting as a point of reference that allows us to appreciate and magnify the valley's gentle slope toward the south and the harshly broken mass of the mountain range. The narrow building consists of two parallel walls of double brick layers and a succession of wooden rafters placed every twenty inches (fifty centimeters), spanning the distance between the two walls and supporting the roof.

Taking advantage of the lengthwise slope of the site, the house is developed on different levels, having only one level in the northern end, three different levels in the center—where the reception areas are located—and two levels in the southern end, the bedroom area.

Above: *The deviation from the orthogonal of the porch columns optically stresses the longitudinal design of the house.*

Opposite Page: *The particular conception of the garden, crossed by transverse lines of bricks, echoes the different levels of the house's longitudinal profile.*

North Elevation

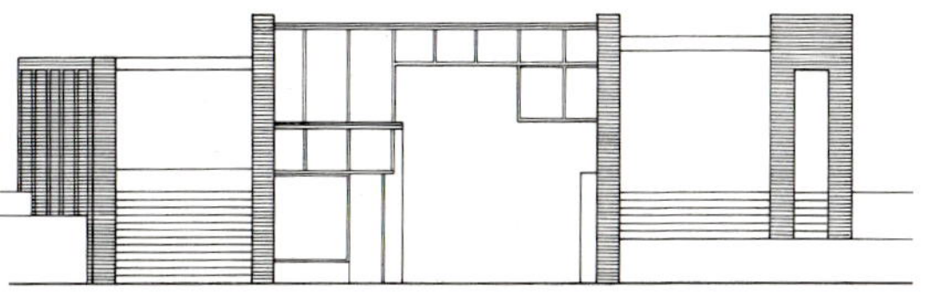

South Elevation

0 1 2 3 4 5m

Site Plan

0   10m

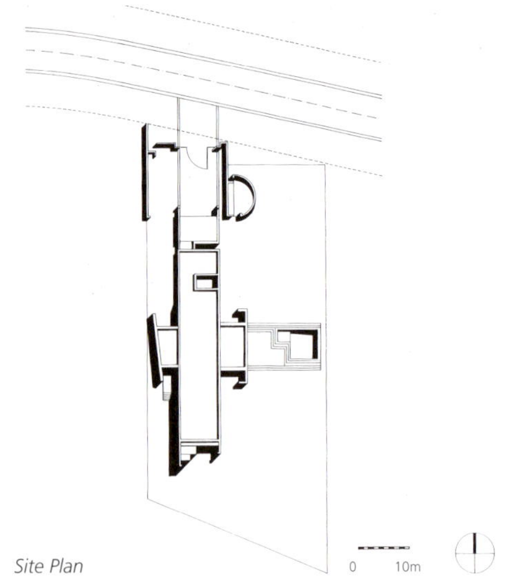

First Floor Plan

0   5m

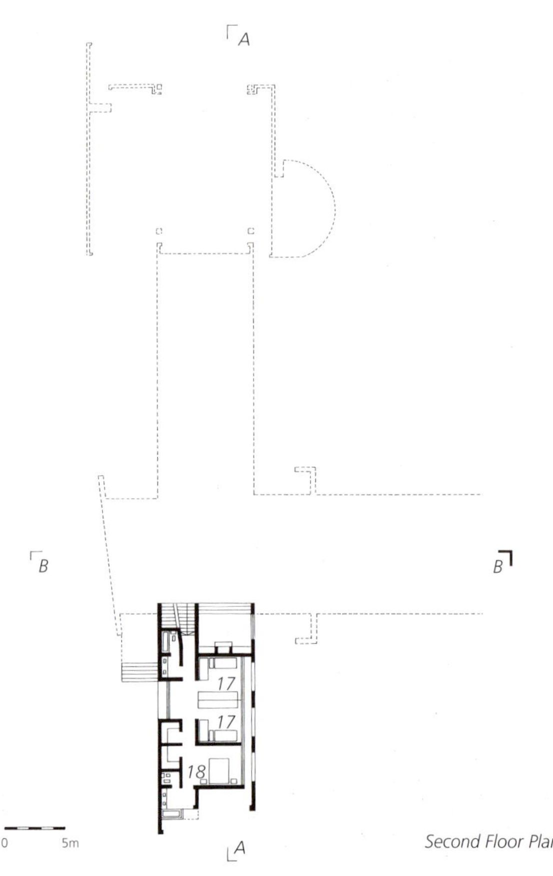

Second Floor Plan

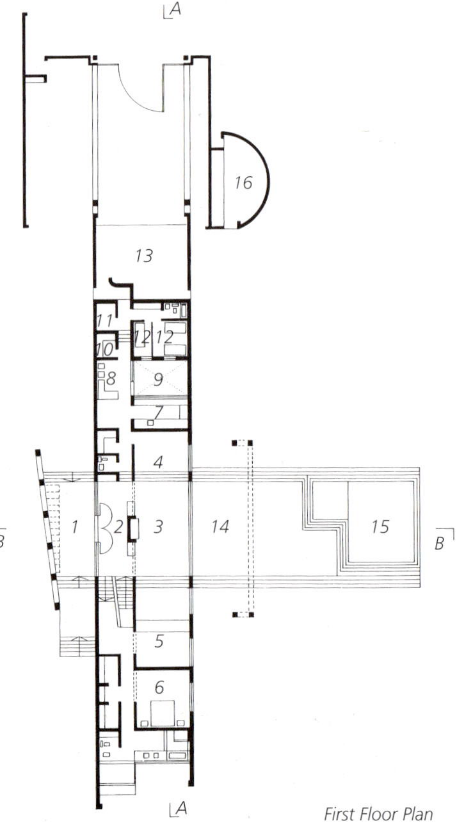

This Page: *The long horizontal line formed by the parallel brick walls establishes a supporting horizon for the cordilleran profile.*

Opposite Page: *The ground plan distinctly expresses the will of achieving the greatest possible length with a relatively modest program.*

This Page: *The walls stretch past the house itself, distinctly asserting the architectural stand and the simplicity of the constructive system.*

Opposite Page: *The swimming pool was set above the terrace level so as to allow a best sunning of the water.*

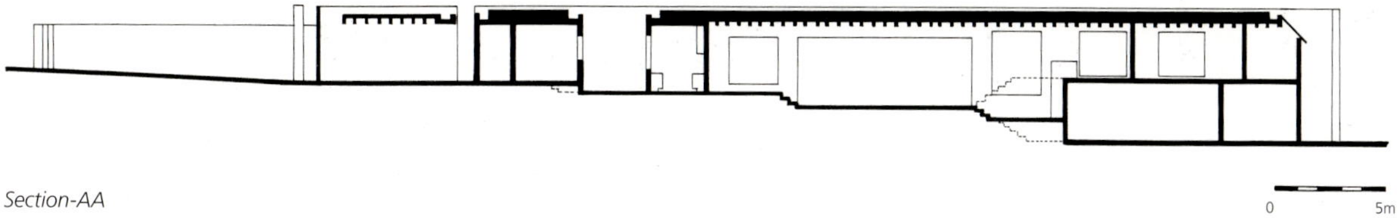

Section-AA

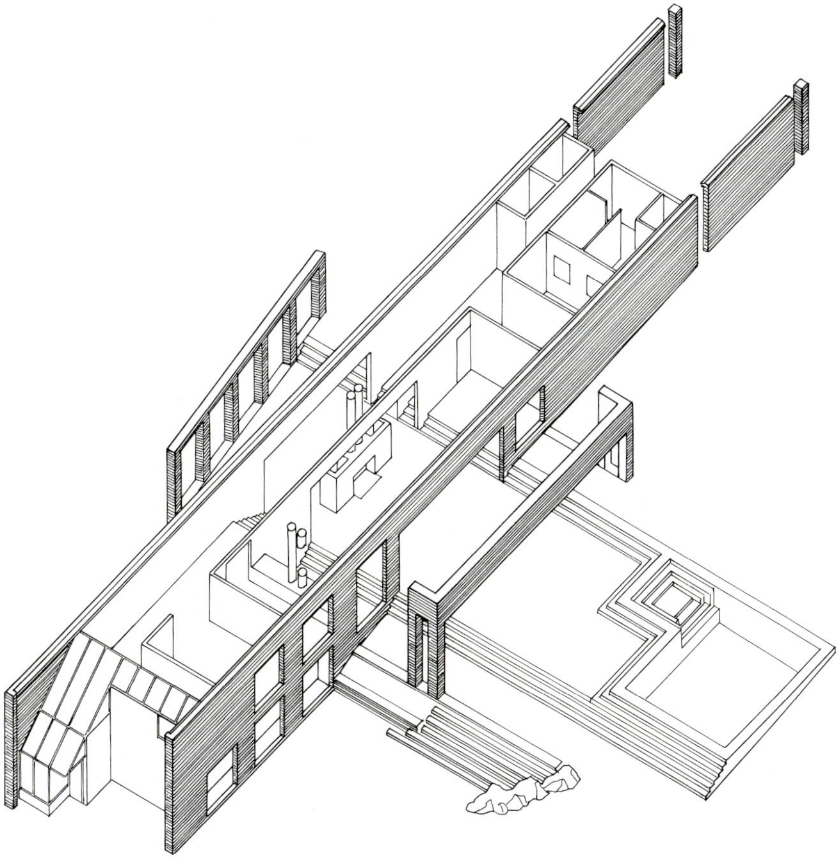

Axonometric View

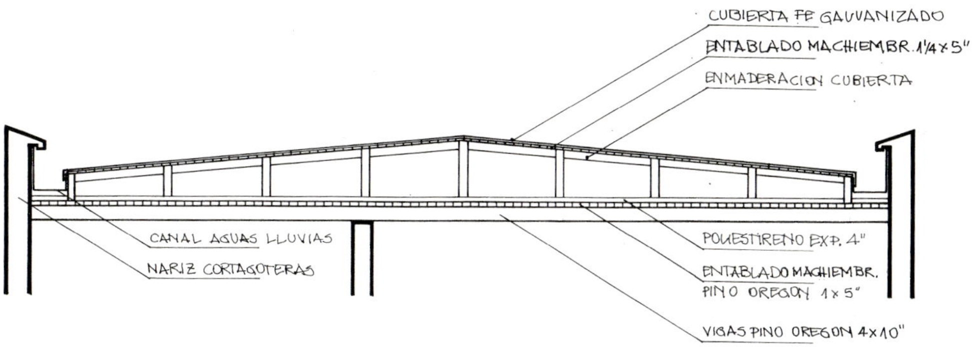

Roof Section

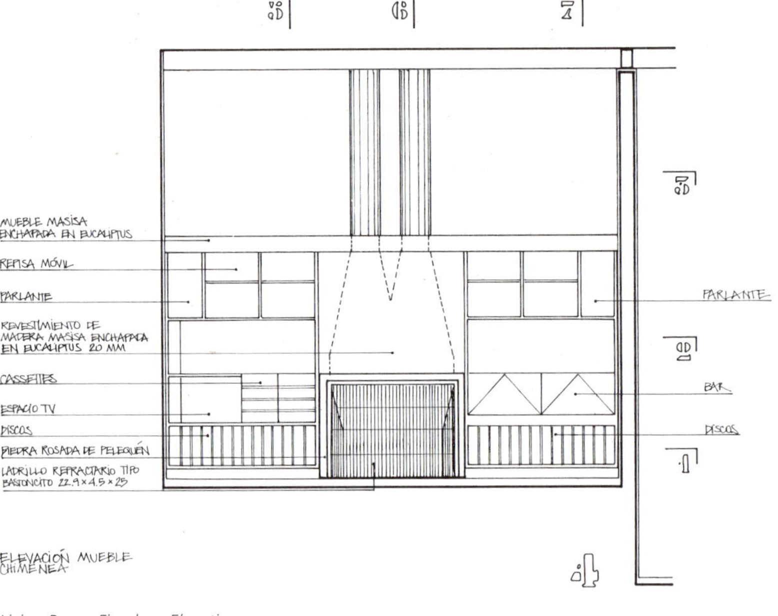

Living Room Fireplace Elevation

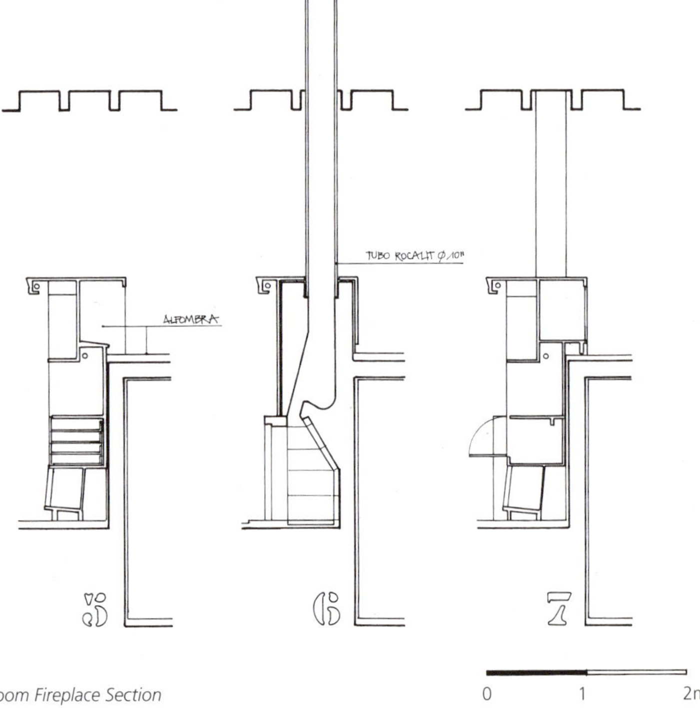

Living Room Fireplace Section

This Page: *The house's system of levels assumes and enhances the north-south slope of the site.*

Opposite Page: *General view of the reception rooms. The different areas, although sharing the same space, become separated, private spaces due to the system of levels.*

Gellona House

Santiago, Chile

Above: *Aerial view of the house showing the strict symmetry of the ground plan, which develops around the large central patio.*

Opposite Page: *Axis of the access with the patio at the far end. The landscaping follows the spirit of the Italian villas.*

The site is, undoubtedly, one of the most spectacular in the city, practically dominating the whole valley of Santiago. With the Andes Cordillera as backdrop, the site sits atop a high plateau and is accessible through soft slopes. These special characteristics of the site—large dimensions, flat surface, access through soft slopes, and its vocation as a watchtower—suggested the idea of the house as an Italian villa standing at the highest spot of the site, its axis oriented toward the center of the view over the city of Santiago.

The access to the house consists of a large patio, flat and symmetrical, with blind walls completely confining the view both toward the valley and the nearest chain of hills and toward the Cordillera. When entering the house, the large opening overlooking the city and the surrounding geography provide a stunning surprise. The height of the walls shaping the patio is not only a function of the dimension of the space, but of allowing just the view of the sky.

Following the style of Italian villas, the house was developed in successive symmetrical terraces that move forward, descending toward, the garden and the view. The program was divided into two main levels, leaving in the upper one the noblest areas—reception rooms and master bedroom—and in the lower story, the children's and guest bedrooms to one side, the service area and carport to the other.

On both sides of the living room, toward the dining room and the master bedroom, two spacious terraces were created, protected from the sun and the wind on three of their sides. The service wing lies to the west, nearer to the public access road. A dry-stone wall toward the north gives the house total privacy.

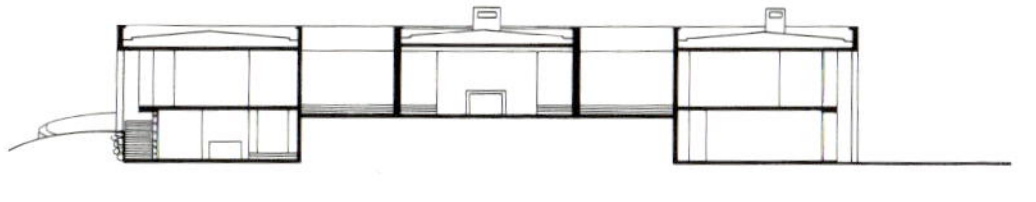

Section A-A

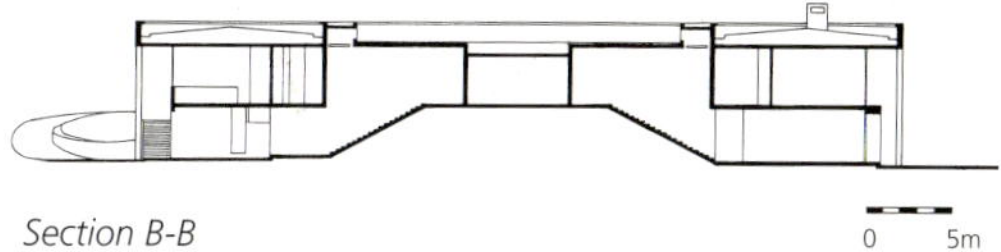

Section B-B

0   5m

Gellona House

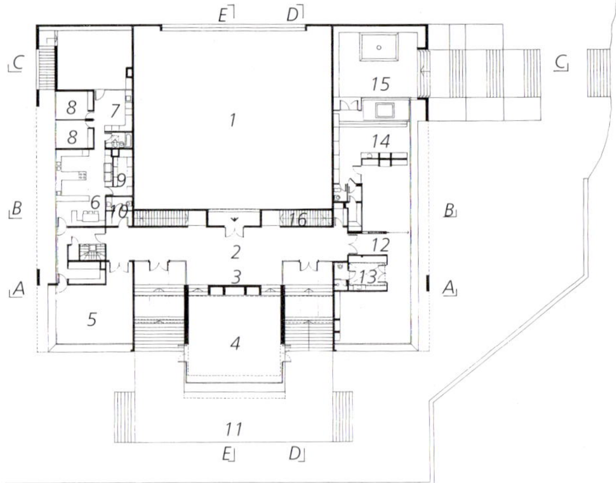

Main Floor Plan

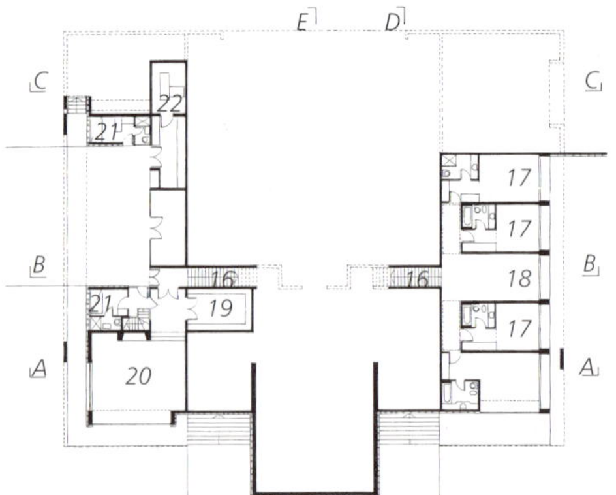

Lower Floor Plan

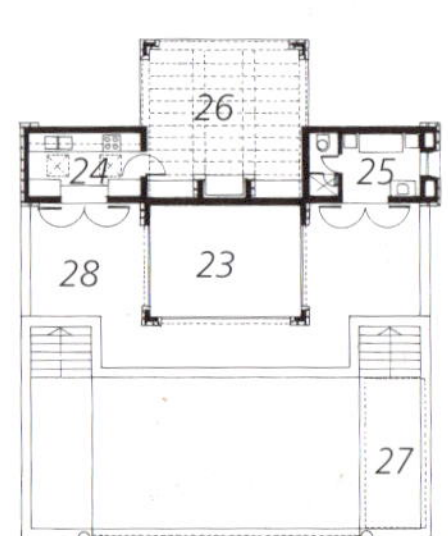

Swimming Pool Pavilion

0   5m

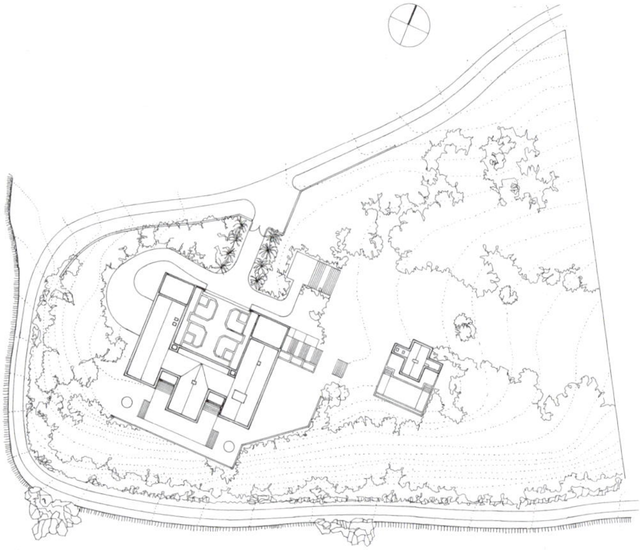

1. Courtyard
2. Entrance
3. Main Hall
4. Living Room
5. Dinning Room
6. Kitchen
7. Laundry
8. Service
9. Larder/Pantry
10. Guest Bathroom
11. Terrace
12. Master Bedroom
13. Closet
14. Main Bathroom
15. Patio
16. Stairs to Lower Level
17. Bedroom
18. Family Room
19. Bar
20. Family Room
21. Service Room
22. Mechanical
23. Pavilion Living Room
24. Kitchenette
25. Dressing Room
26. Roofed Terrace
27. Swimming Pool
28. Swimming Pool Terrace

Site Plan

0   40m

This Page: *The main access patio and the swimming-pool pavilion follow the "Acropolis" nature of the site.*

Opposite Page: *Due to its particular geographic characteristics, the place used to be a popular spot for practicing "delta-wings" sport (hang gliding). The ground plan is an unequivocal evocation of that use.*

This Page: *The planning of the garden and the proportions of the various exterior works are in perfect tuning with the status of the house and the unique character of the site.*

Opposite Page: *The treatment of the façades was simplified to the utmost, thus accentuating the unusual scale of the planes of walls, beams and windows.*

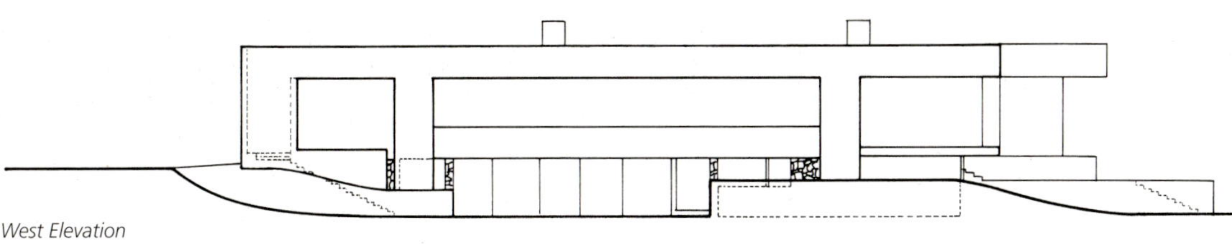

West Elevation

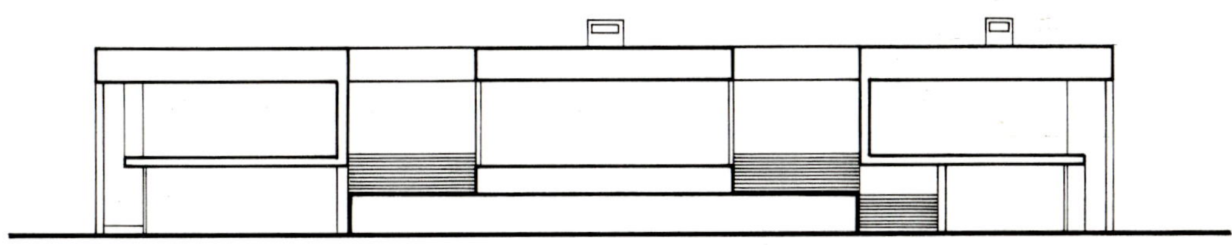

South Elevation

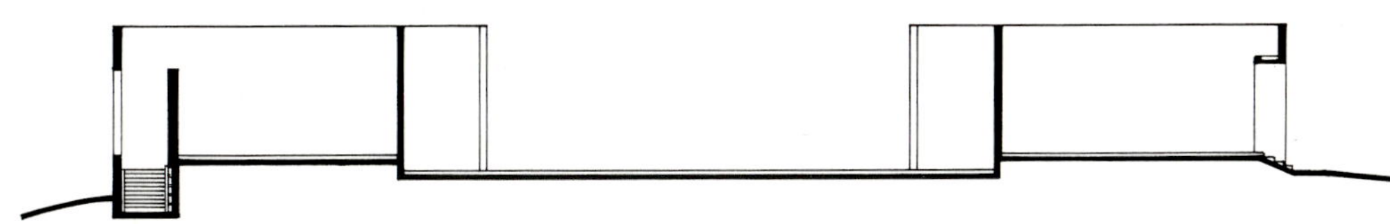

Section C-C

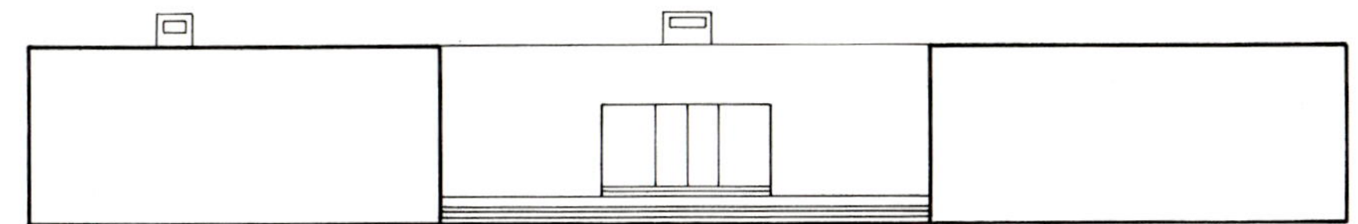

North Elevation

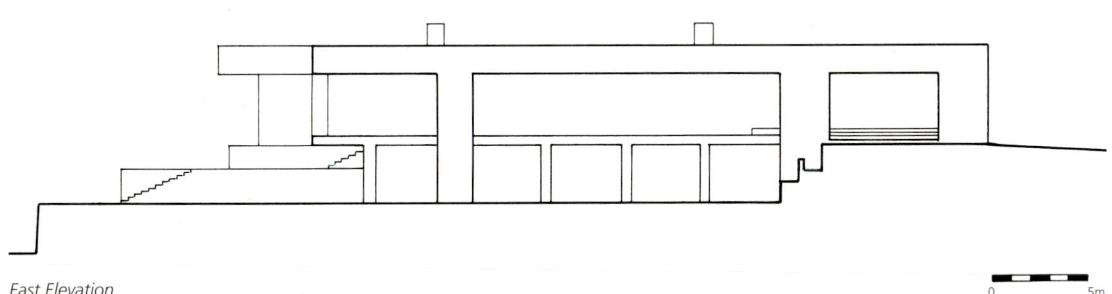

East Elevation

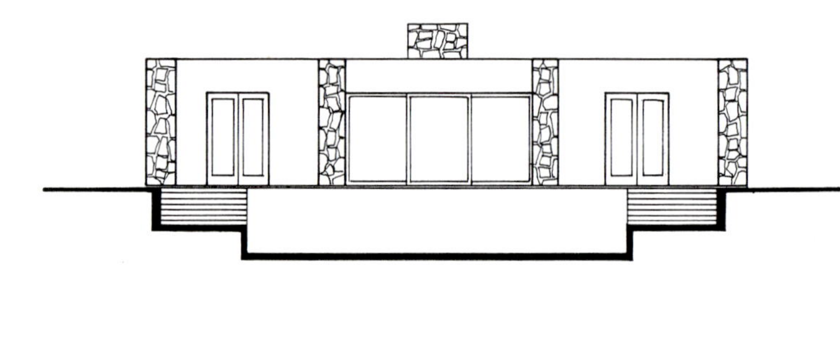

Swimming Pool Pavilion Section A-A

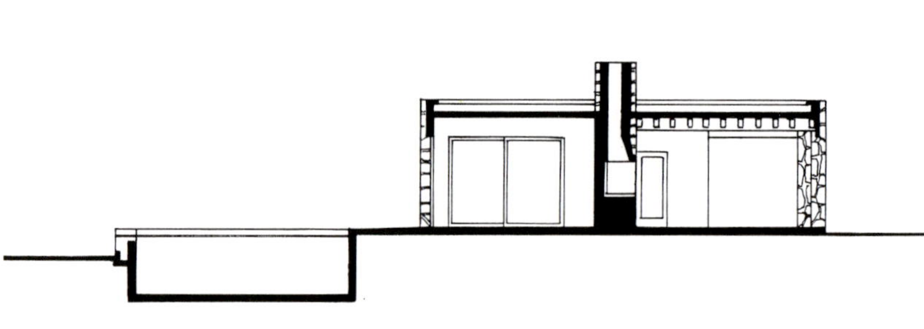

Swimming Pool Pavilion Section B-B

Swimming Pool Pavilion Section C-C

Swimming Pool Pavilion Section D-D

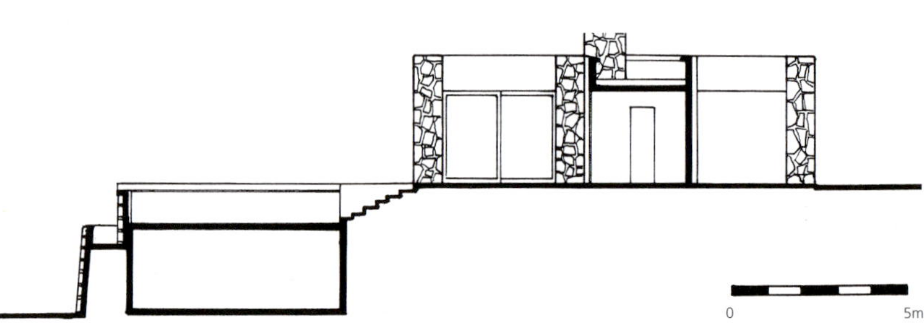

Swimming Pool Pavilion Section E-E

This Page: *The large access gallery is in harmony with the magnitude of the house. The interior design belongs to the proprietor, not the architects.*

Opposite Page: *The bottom left photograph clearly conveys the sensation of being suspended over the city of Santiago.*

Matte House

Zapallar, Chile

Above: The swimming pool hangs over the resort bay, giving an impression of continuity with the sea. Two tall pines frame the view.

Opposite Page: The house was conceived as a geography of turrets and walls merging with the site. The effect is emphasized by the extensive use of local stone.

Set on a beautiful spot in a seaside resort, above a fishing cove on the western end of Zapallar Beach, the site was part of the garden and access to the beach of an old manor demolished after the 1970 earthquake. Apart from broken and profuse vegetation, and gigantic old pine trees, the site also had an infrastructure of terraces, walls, and ramps. A turret perched on a large rock served as a lookout tower toward the bay and the beach. All of these structures were constructed out in the typical stone used in the old buildings of the resort.

One of the first basic decisions taken as part of the architectural proposition was the incorporation of the entire infrastructure of walls, terraces, ramps, and turret into the new project. Thus the house would reveal the place and the landscape in the same way it revealed them to the architect the first time he had visited it. The melding of the new constructions and the old remains allowed the project to be embedded in time, dissolving into the landscape as a ruin would.

The project proposed a geography of three low, thick turrets echoing the broken, abrupt anatomy of the Chilean coast. A group of slender towers thrust upward into the air contrasts with trunks of the huge pine trees that are an essential characteristic of the site. These towers established a rhythm defining the elements of the program. The living areas are arranged in platforms resting on the towers and thrown out into space like tree branches. The juxtaposition of only two materials, stone and glass, makes for an unencumbered and austere building that continues, intertwines, and reflects the topography and vegetation of the area.

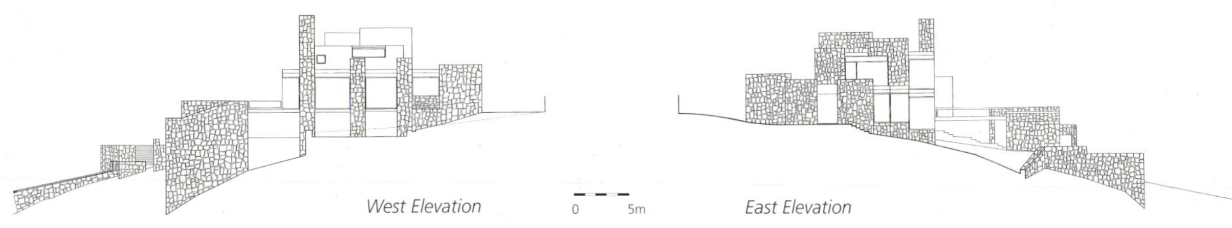

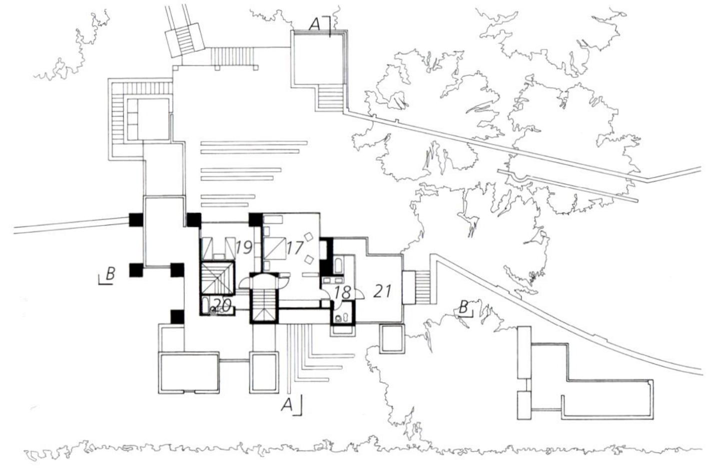

First Floor Plan

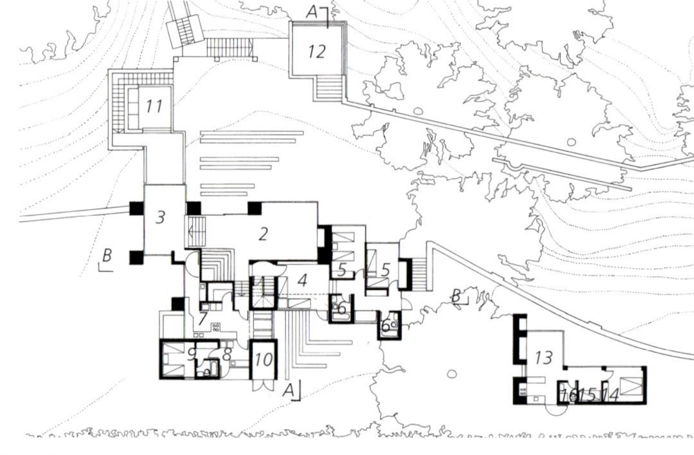

Second Floor Plan

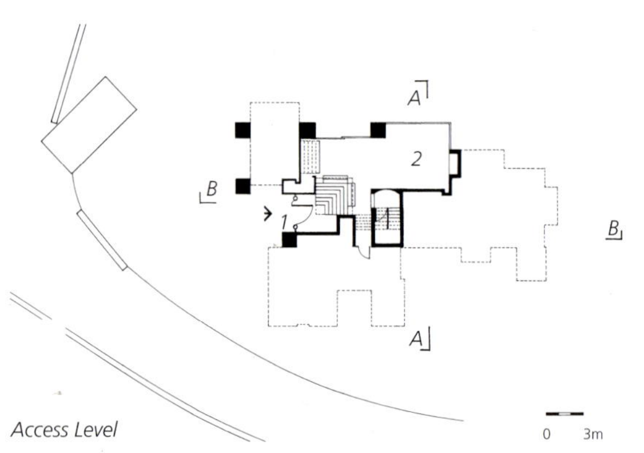

Access Level

0   3m

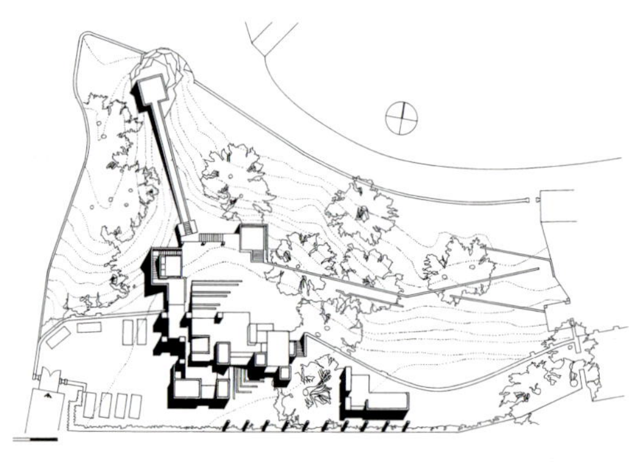

Site Plan

0   15m

1. Entrance
2. Living Room
3. Dining Room
4. Family Living Room
5. Bedroom
6. Bathroom
7. Kitchen
8. Laundry
9. Service Bedroom
10. Mechanical
11. Barbecue Tower
12. Swimming Pool
13. Butler's Living Room/Kitchen
14. Butler's Main Bedroom
15. Butler's Bedroom
16. Butler's Bathroom
17. Master Bedroom
18. Bathroom
19. Guest Bedroom
20. Guest Bathroom
21. Terrace

This Page: *The house camouflages itself with the splendidly wooded landscape, while the stones and towers assert its presence.*

Opposite Page: *The ground plans clearly show the adaptation of the architecture to the turrets and walls-vestiges, just as to the trees covering the place.*

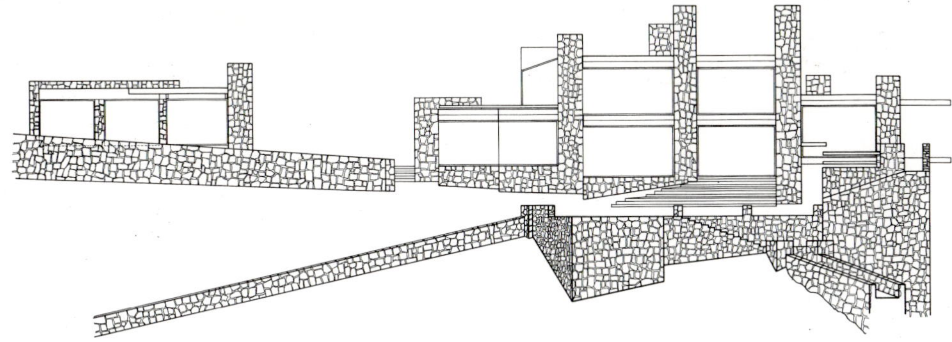

North Elevation

Axonometric View

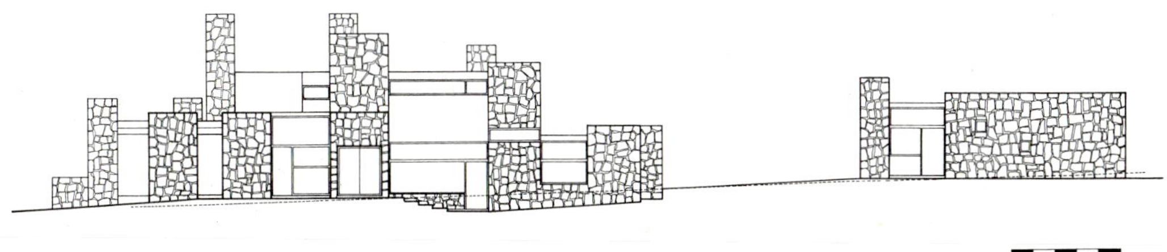

South Elevation

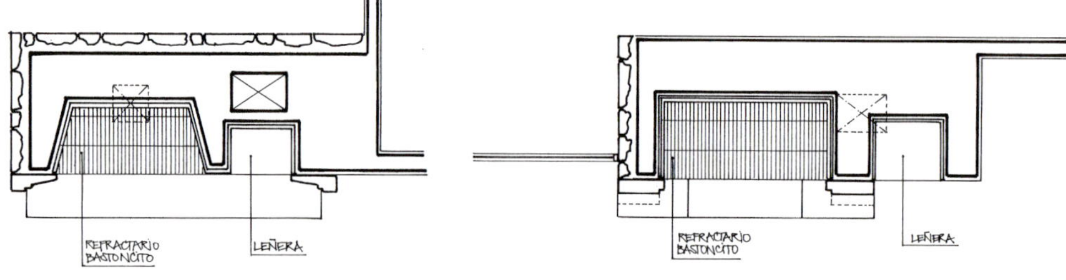

Living Room/Master Bedroom Fireplace Plans

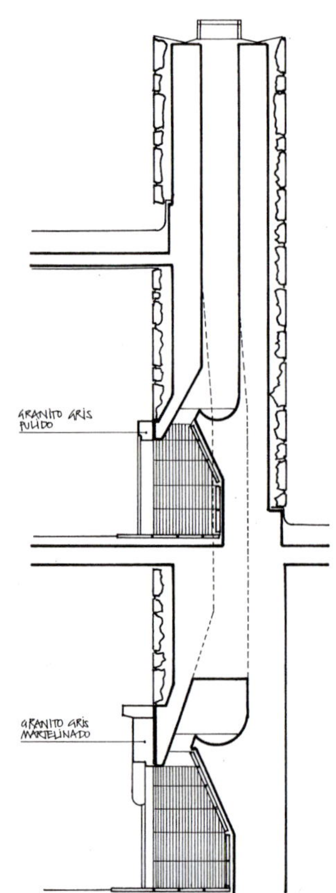

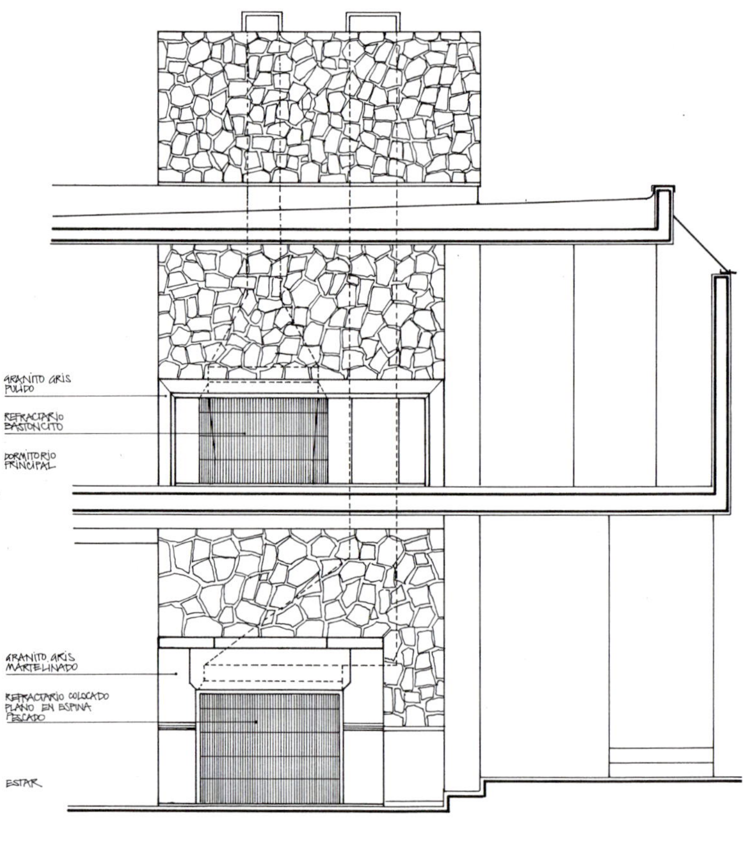

Living Room/Master Bedroom Fireplace Section and Elevation

Orrego House

El Pangue, Chile

Located on a beautiful spot at the seashore, the house lies halfway between the traditional beach resorts of Zapallar and Cachagua, and faces "El Pangue," a marvelous rocky bay. The site, of about 54,000 square feet (5,000 square meters), is set on a hillside between the new and old roads linking the seaside resorts.

Towards the south, halfway between the site and the sea, there is a screen of huge eucalyptus, filtering the view across to the sea and rocks and turning the sunset into a magic sight. The owners, a very sensitive couple, wanted the house to be a true turning point in their lives, and they were placing high hopes in the enterprise, to the extent of describing it as "The Maison Sourire."

The architectural stance establishes a geographical counterpoint with the filter-like screen of eucalyptus, resulting in a linear nature. Moreover, it provides the house total privacy, isolating it from the noise coming from the road running along the upper side of the site.

To achieve this effect, an actual "street" seven feet (two meters) wide was created. Formed by a double wall connecting all the rooms—and acting as an acoustic and visual barrier against the pollution from the road—this street is open to the sky, roofed with double-sealed glass. Along the "street," different rooms form a "town," with intermediate open spaces resembling small squares for relaxation and meditation.

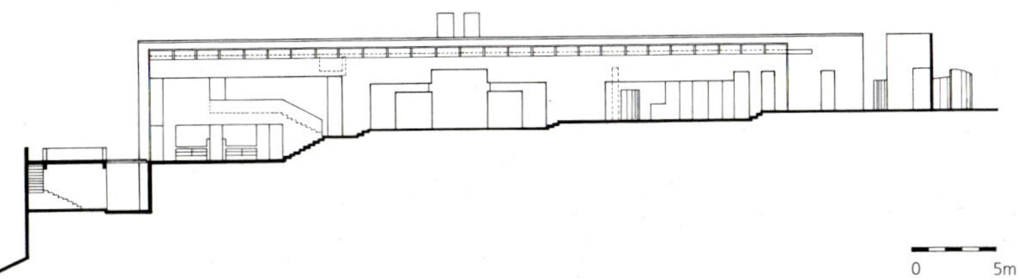

Section A-A

Above: *The long street, forming the spine of the house and constituting the connecting element of the whole, ends on the south in a turret, which dramatizes the descent to the site.*

Opposite Page: *General view of the variety of volumes forming the house, bound together by the contrasting linear street.*

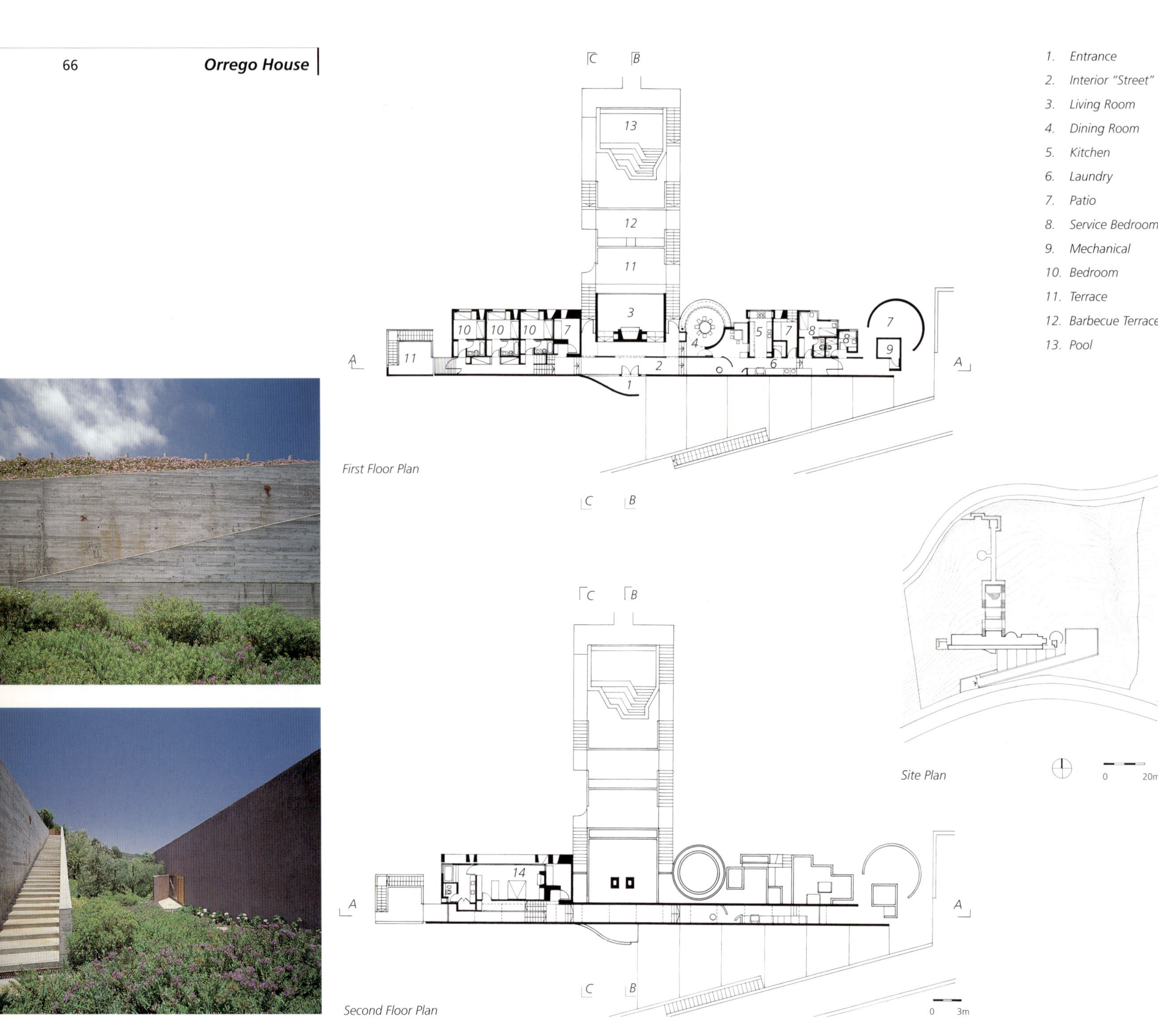
13
12
11
3
10 10 10 7
11
7
4
5 7 8
6 8
9
A A
C B
First Floor Plan
C B
14
8
A A
C B
Second Floor Plan
0   3m
Site Plan
0   20m
1. Entrance
2. Interior "Street"
3. Living Room
4. Dining Room
5. Kitchen
6. Laundry
7. Patio
8. Service Bedroom
9. Mechanical
10. Bedroom
11. Terrace
12. Barbecue Terrace
13. Pool

This Page: *The three lower photographs show the street with its different levels. The skylight structure also serves the purpose of stabilizing the walls laterally.*

Opposite Page: *The system of terraces and swimming pool, laid out perpendicular to the house, is also the element that connects the upper and lower roads flanking the site.*

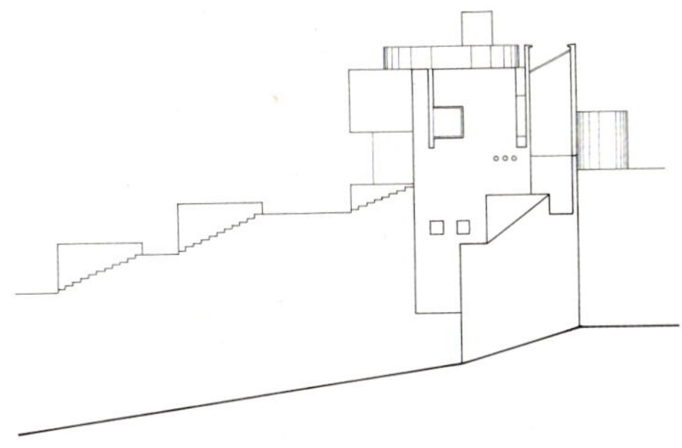

West Elevation

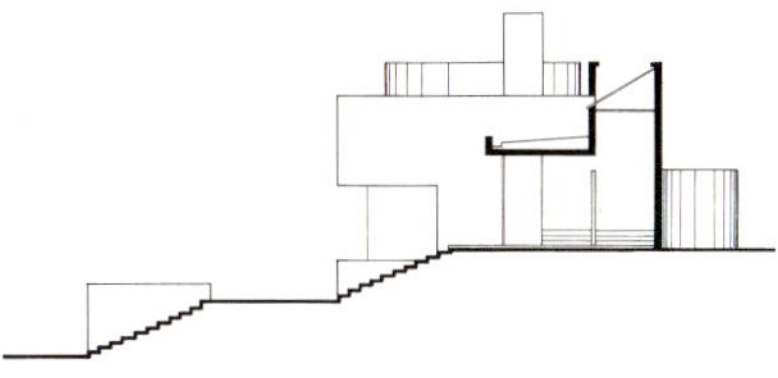

Section C-C

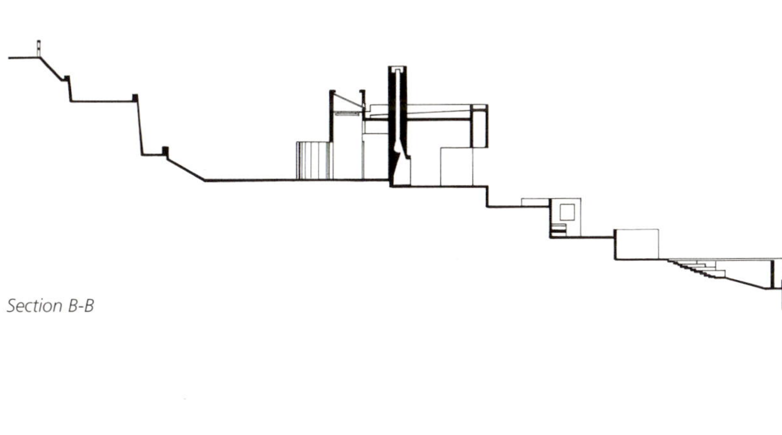

Section B-B

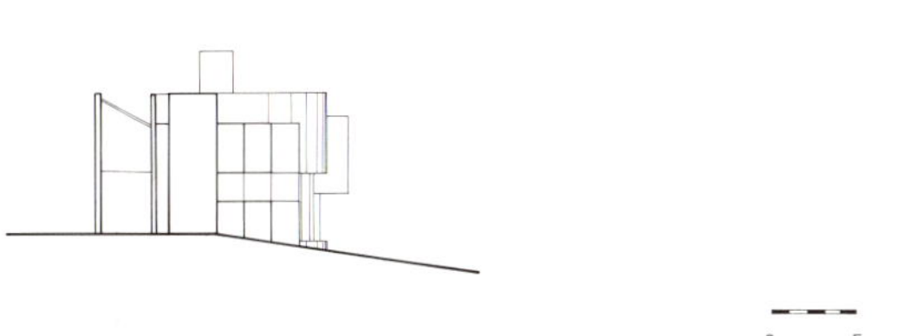

East Elevation

0   5m

This page: *The construction materials were reduced to a strict minimum, leaving all eloquence to space and light.*

Opposite Page: *The inner wall system of trimmings is determined by the importance of the rooms it gives access to, in this case the main living room.*

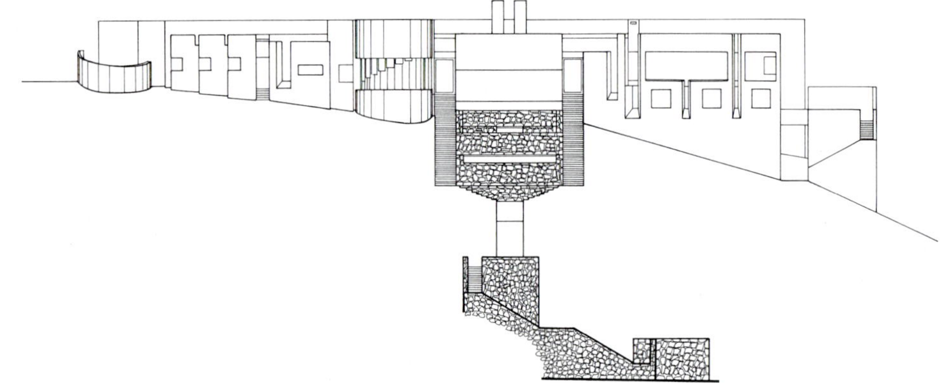

North Elevation

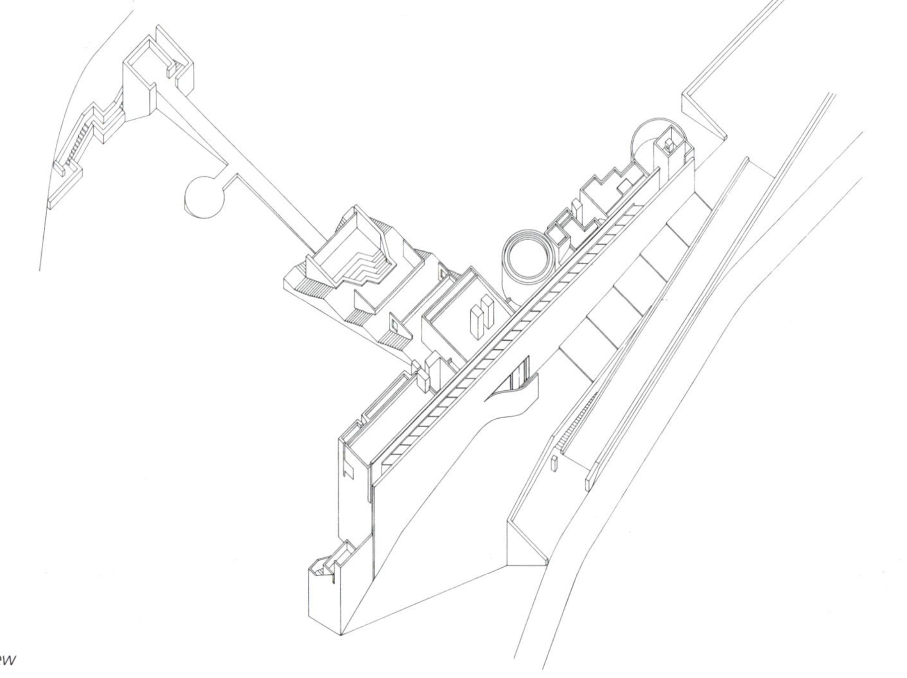

Axonometric View

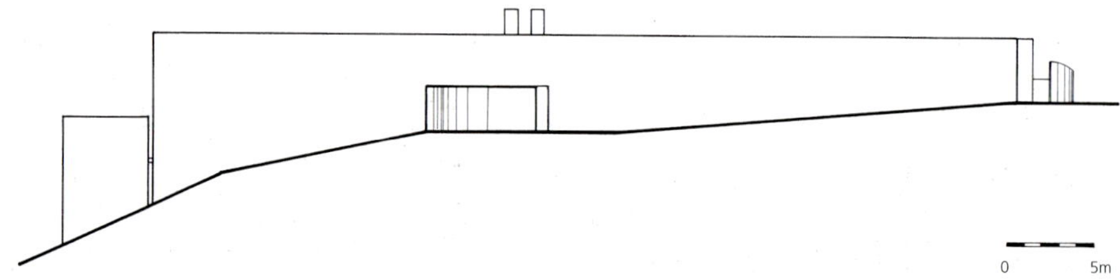

South Elevation

This Page: *The master bedroom's upper photograph, dominates the view toward the ocean through a screen of eucalyptus. Sunset behind this filter becomes a magic sight.*

Opposite Page: *The impenetrability of the house with regard to the road contrasts with the openness of its volumes and terraces toward the sea.*

This Page: *One of a few small areas open to the sky yet granting to our client complete isolation from the rest of the house dwellers.*

Opposite Page: *The terraces and swimming pool, in exposed concrete, share the sternness of materials characteristic of the entire work.*

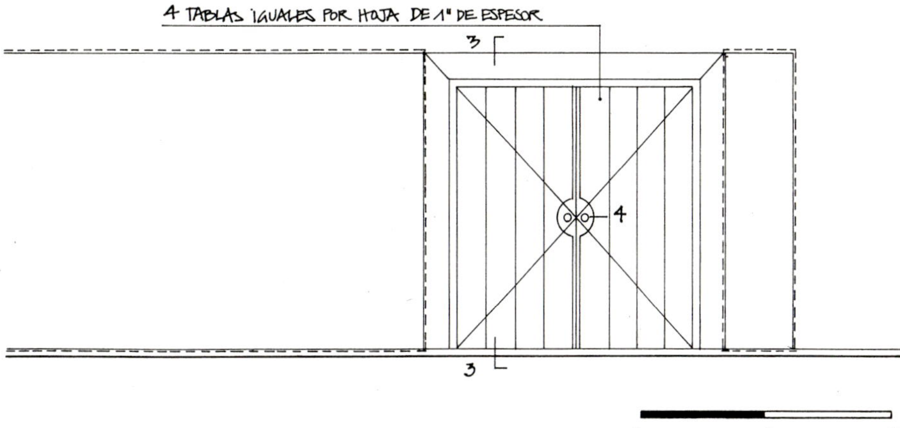

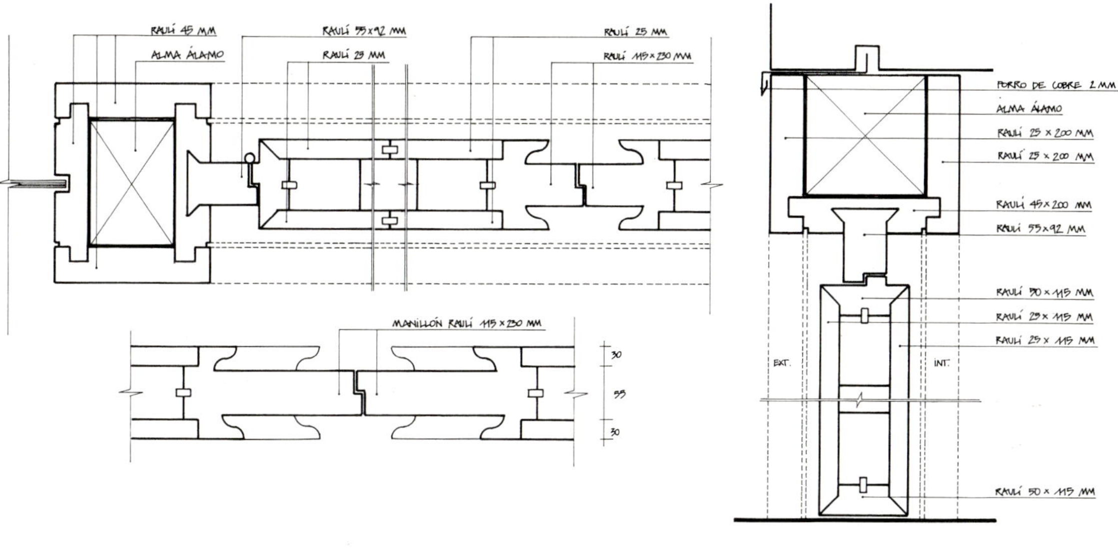

Access Door Details

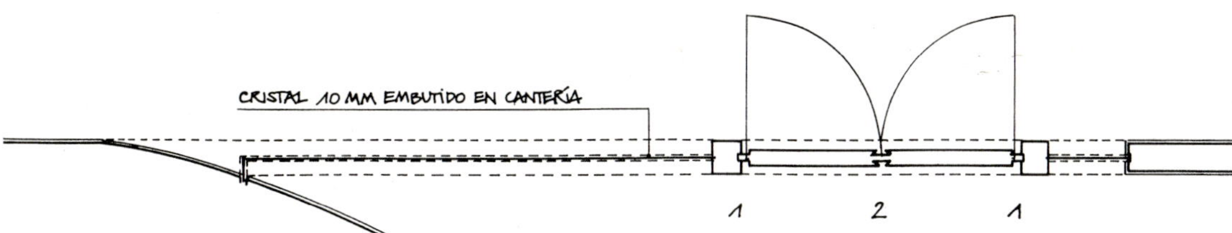

Elisa House

Santiago, Chile

The site, 54,000 square feet (5,000 square meters) in area and located at the feet of the Manquehue Hill, is sharply inclined toward the east and is densely covered with native Chilean trees, especially quillayes, litres, and espinos. The view toward the hills and to the Andes range of mountains—at an angle of practically 180 degrees—is spectacular.

The characteristics of the topography, the vegetation, the surrounding views, and the requirement of providing the house with an heliport led us to the general scheme of building three large "trays" of exposed concrete supported by parallel, stone-covered buttress walls. They make the house "stand on tiptoe" on the slope without changing the natural ground level of the existing trees. These "trays," arranged according to the direction of the contour lines, and the walls, perpendicular to them, are cut out to allow the trees to pierce and determine the perimeter of the house. Thus the tallest and leafiest quillay in the site goes through the interior of the reception area, forming a patio totally surrounded by glass, which in turn allows a spatial interconnection among the different levels. The interior spaces are delimited by large panes of glass with no visible frames, allowing a spectacular and uninterrupted view of the mountains and surrounding vegetation.

In order to enhance the importance of this building and, at the same time, to closely bind the "trays" to the topography, a greenhouse surrounded by a ramp was built to the south. To the east, a system of wide ramps connect the three main levels of the house and those of the garden and terraces.

Above: *Aerial view of the house showing the painstaking adaptation to the site's topography and native vegetation.*

Opposite Page: *Out of consideration for the topography, the garden comprises a geography of steps that slips under the house to surface at the back.*

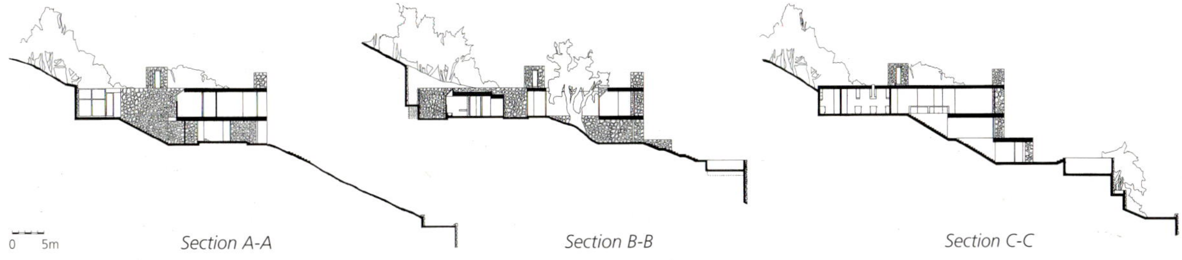

Elisa House

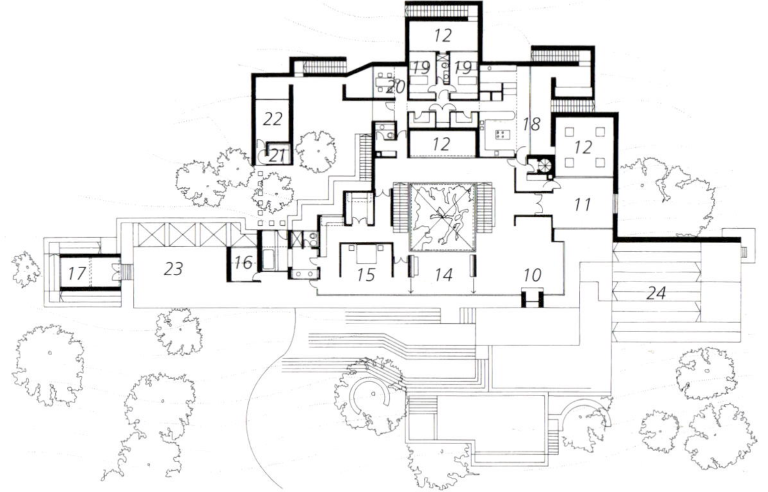

Main Level

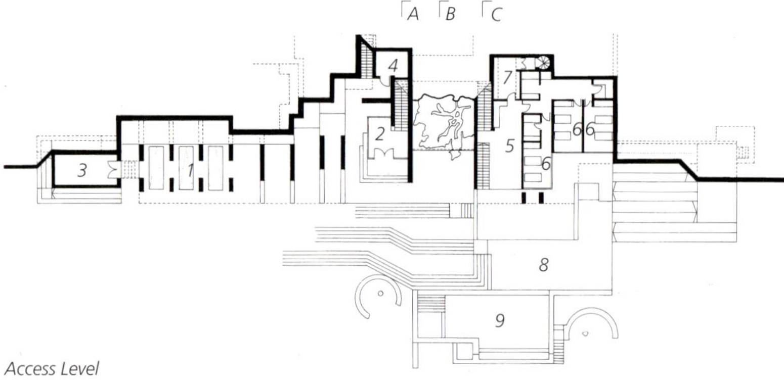

Access Level

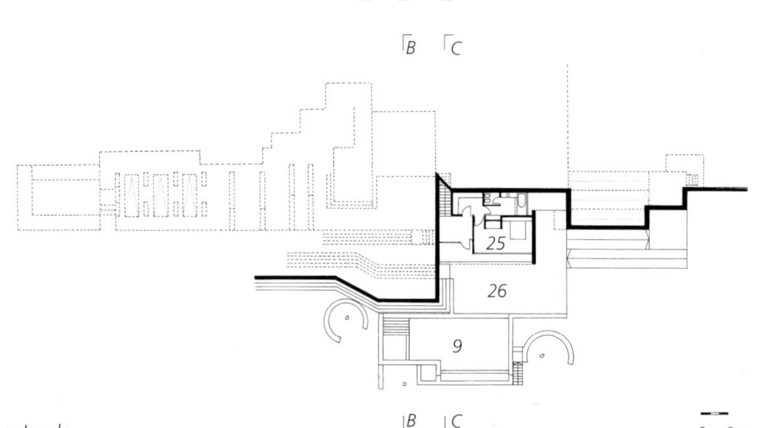

Lower Level

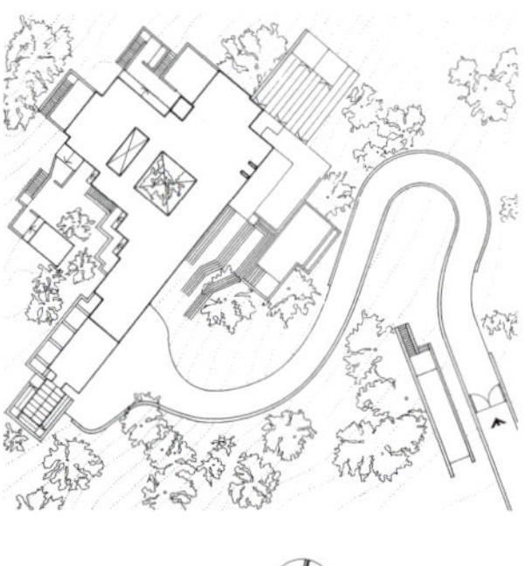

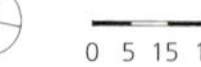

Site Plan

1. Carport
2. Entrance Hall
3. Storage
4. Mechanical
5. Family Room
6. Bedroom
7. Cave
8. Terrace
9. Pool
10. Living Room
11. Dining Room
12. Patio
13. Gallery
14. Studio
15. Master Bedroom
16. Atelier
17. Green House
18. Kitchen
19. Service Bedroom
20. Service Living Room
21. Sauna
22. Fitting Room
23. Terrace
24. Ramps

0   3m

0 5 15 15m

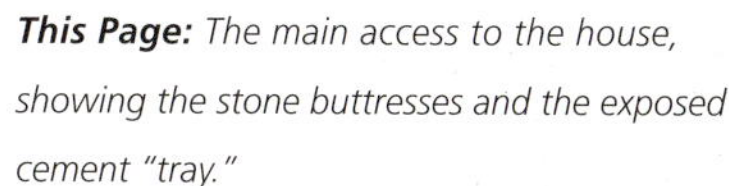

This Page: *The main access to the house, showing the stone buttresses and the exposed cement "tray."*

Opposite Page: *Drawings and photographs show the careful adaptation of architecture to vegetation, to the extent of making the most important tree to pierce the house at its core.*

This Page: *The upper photograph shows a five-hundred-year-old tree (litre), which constitutes the only art piece decorating the room.*

Opposite Page: *The axonometric drawing clearly shows our stand as to extend architecture to the entire site.*

East Elevation

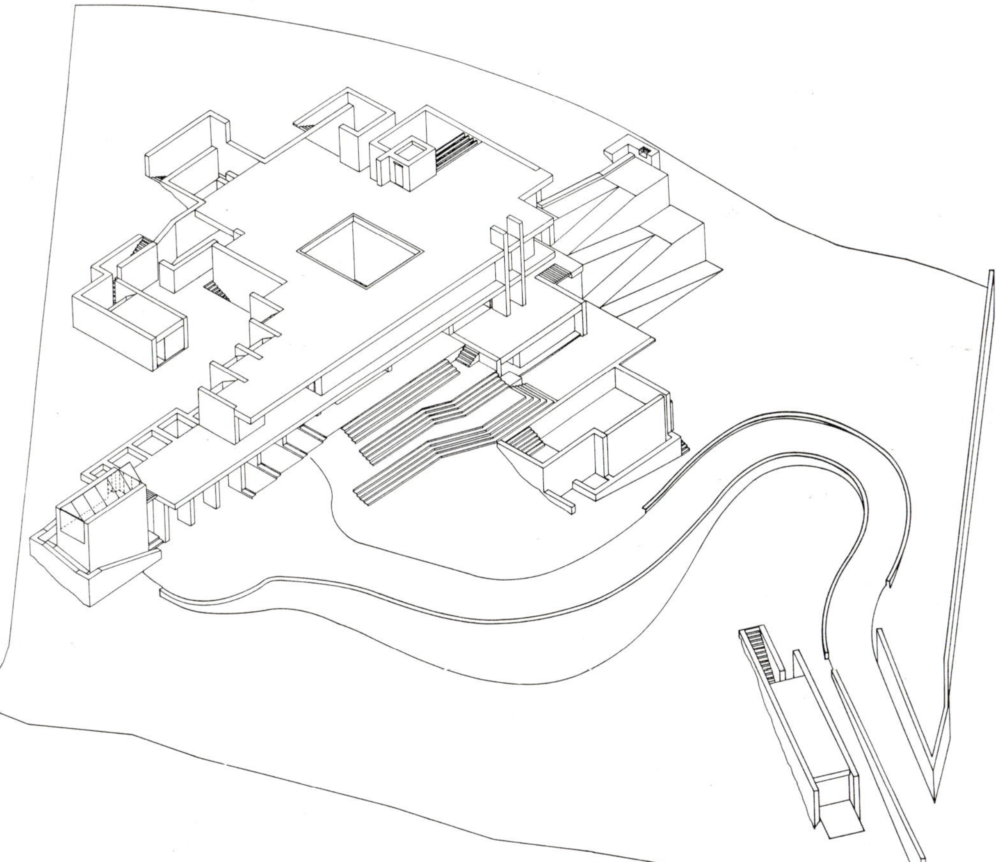

Axonometric View

Elisa House

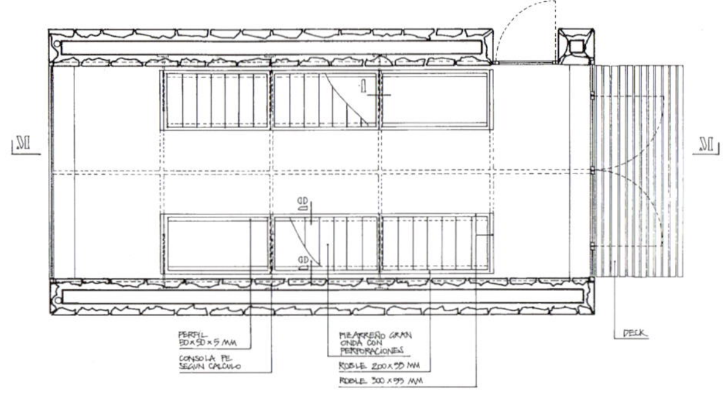

Green House Plan

0 0.5 1m

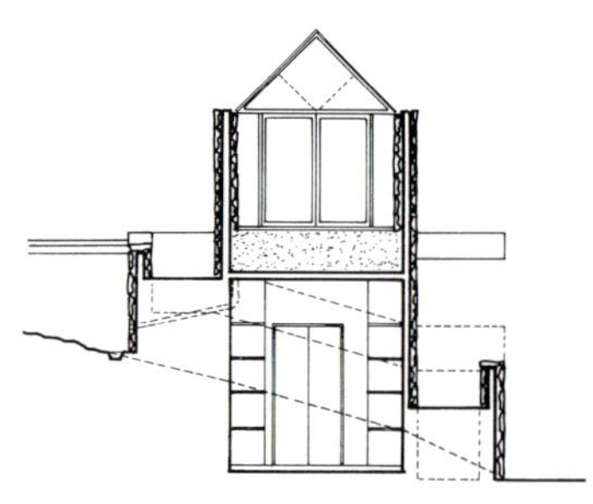

Section Through Green House and Cellar

0 1 2 3m

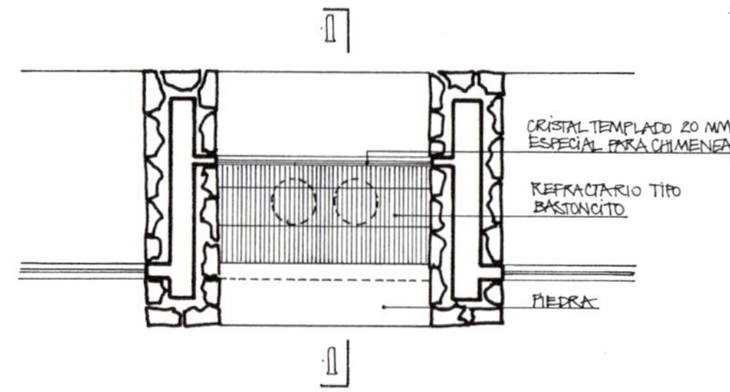

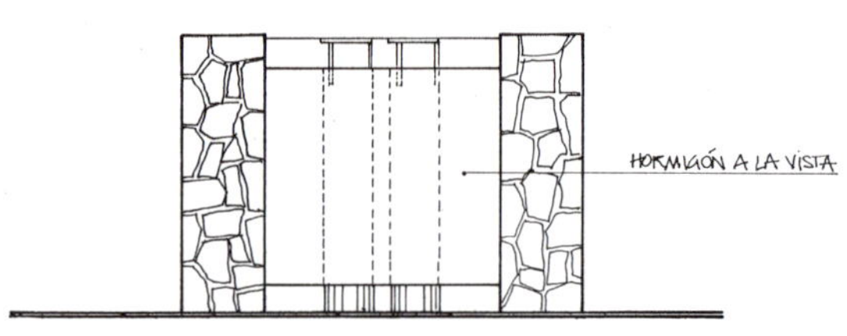

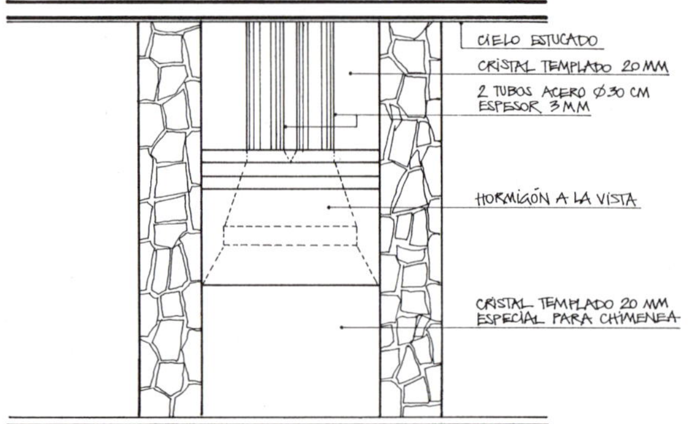

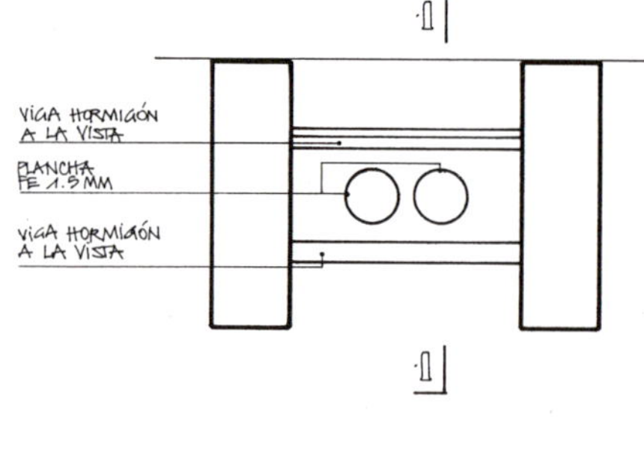

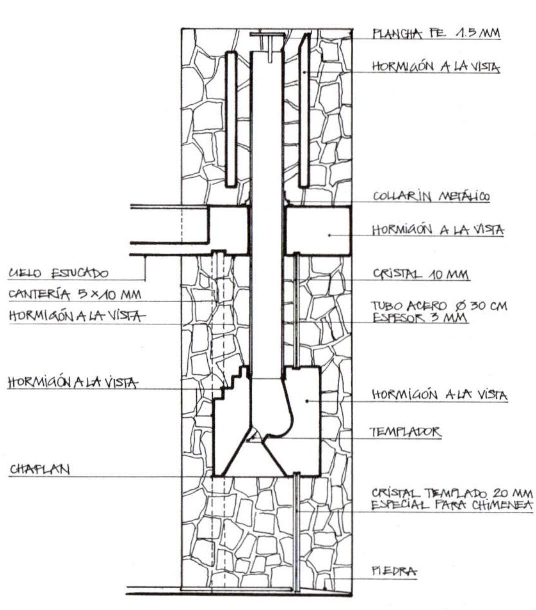

Living Room Fireplace Plans, Elevation, and Section

0 1m

La Cumbre House

Santiago, Chile

Above: *The interplay of volumes and the consistent use of exposed concrete blocks as sole material, strongly contrast with the landscape in which the work is inserted.*

Opposite Page: *The floor plan's spiral development appears with great strength in the general interplay of volumes of the house, forming a dramatic contrast with its back of hills.*

This house is set in the highest portion of a neighborhood located at the feet of a chain of mountains towering over Santiago. The 10,800-square-foot (1,000-square-meter) site sharply inclines toward the street and is surrounded by magnificent native trees, giving shelter within its limits to a pair of very impressive specimens. The Manquehue hill stands directly behind the site.

The house was commissioned to us by a very young couple—of a rather unusual sensibility—with two children. They wanted an especially rich architecture, yet minimalist in finish; moreover, the spatial distribution needed to provide independence to different areas of the house without losing the unity of the whole or sacrificing the good relationship with the still-small children. In accord with the owners—and to make the house more sparing and straightforward—cement blocks and pre-fabricated slabs were used for the entire house. The materials were left exposed both in the interior and the exterior.

The project involved creating a large central space running the entire height of the building. Around this central space, the four different areas of the house were arranged in a spiral path, with a quarter-story difference between each. A staircase revolves inside the large central space, whose railing, based on a wall suspended in the air, both unites the spaces and grants them independence. The space of the staircase is crowned by a great skylight bathing all the rooms of the house in light. The double-height living room connects spatially with the dining room and study that constitutes the last level of the house.

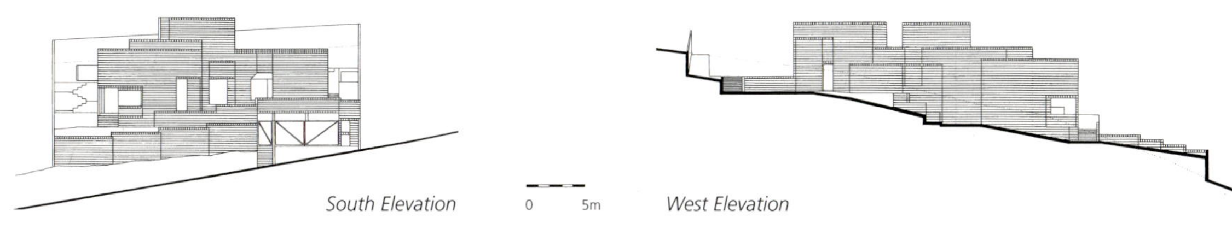

South Elevation   0   5m   *West Elevation*

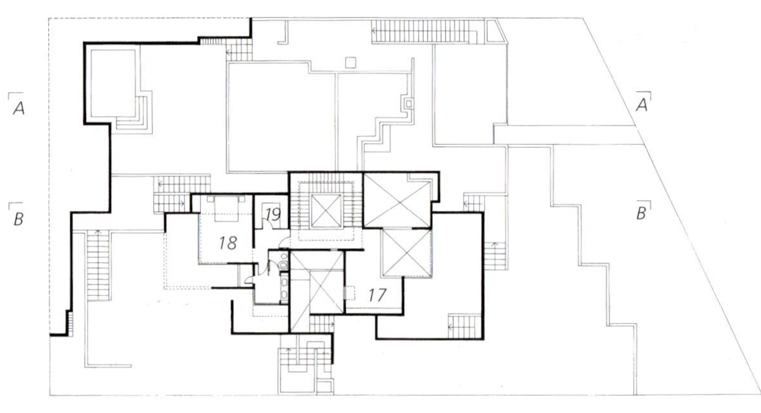

Second Floor Plan

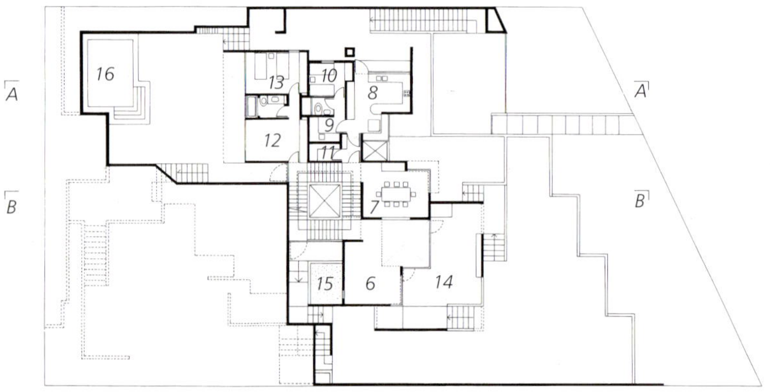

First Floor Plan

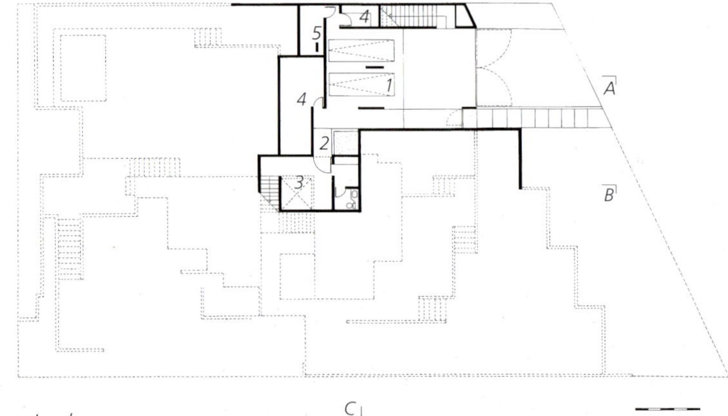

Access Level

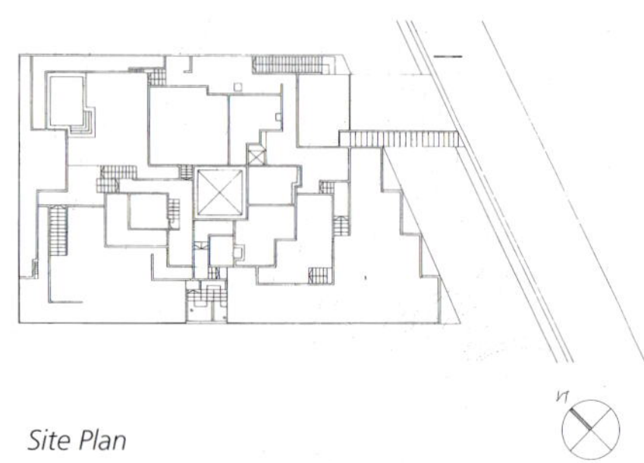

Site Plan

1. Carport
2. Entrance
3. Entrance Hall
4. Storage
5. Mechanical
6. Living Room
7. Dining Room
8. Kitchen
9. Laundry
10. Service Bedroom
11. Pantry
12. Family Room
13. Bedroom
14. Terrace
15. Patio
16. Pool
17. Studio
18. Master Bedroom
19. Walk-in Closet

0   5m

This Page: *These photographs show the creation of intermediate spaces that enlarge the rooms, measure out the landscape, and create a continuous interplay of lights and shadows.*

Opposite Page: *The photographs illustrate how the architecture invades the site in its entirety.*

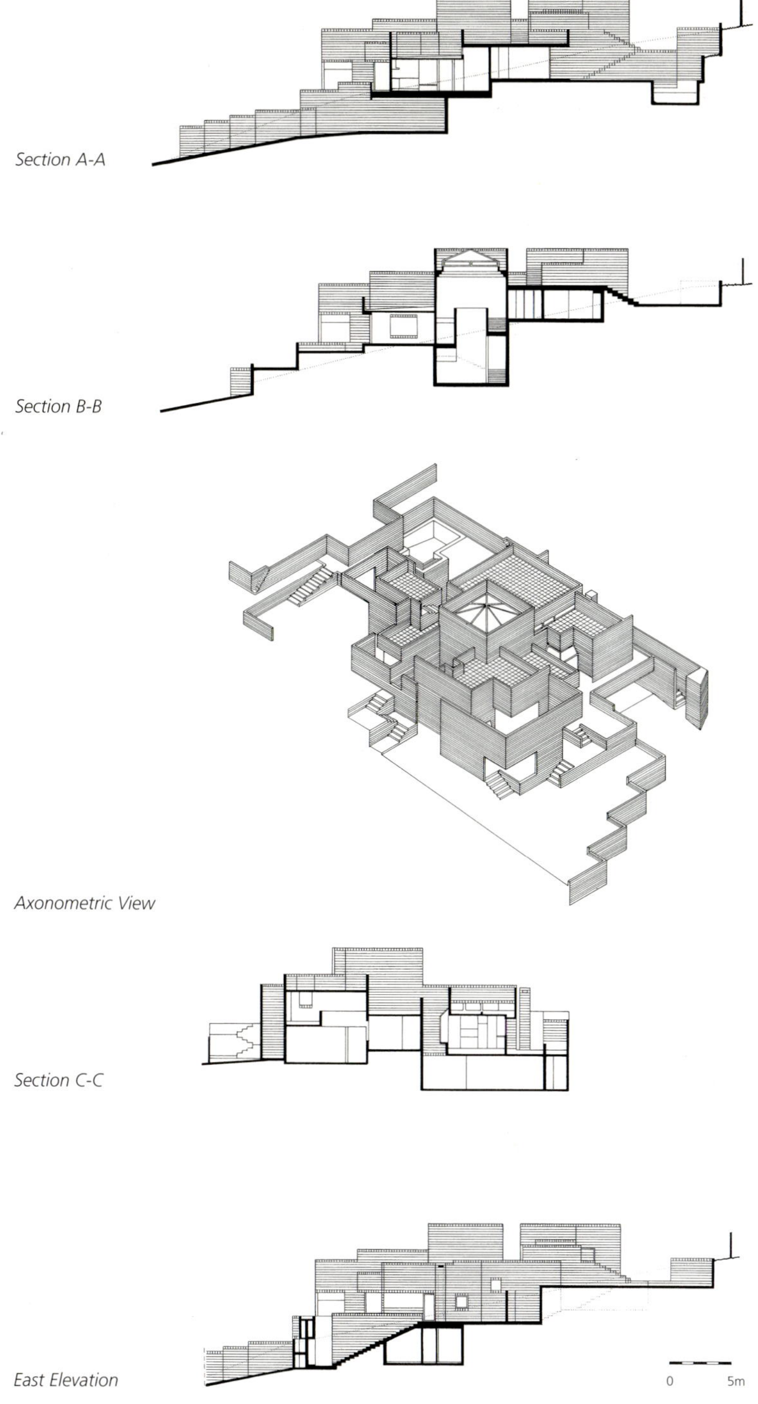

Section A-A

Section B-B

Axonometric View

Section C-C

East Elevation

This Page: *The axonometric drawing gives account of how the architecture rotates and expands itself, starting from the central hall covered with glass.*

Opposite Page: *The intermediate spaces, changes in level, and consistent use of concrete blocks give great unity and spatial richness to the house.*

This and Opposite Page: *Detail of the large central hall around which the different rooms revolve. This space dramatizes the displacements and grants different degrees of privacy to the areas it distributes. The height, light and generosity of this space bestow on the house a status exceeding its modest dimensions.*

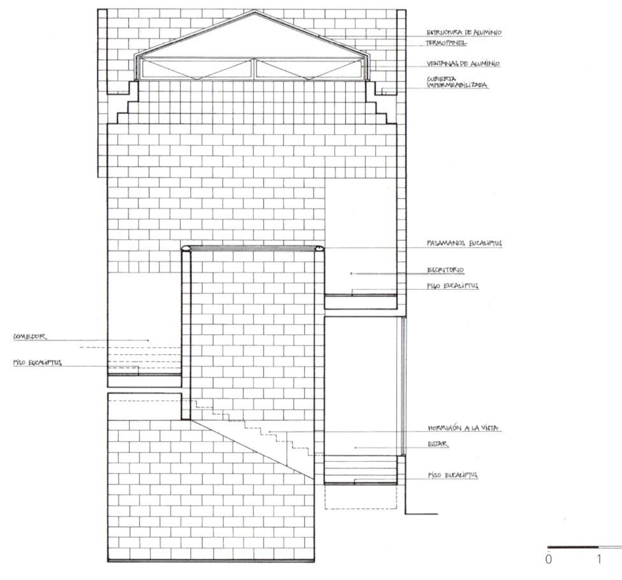

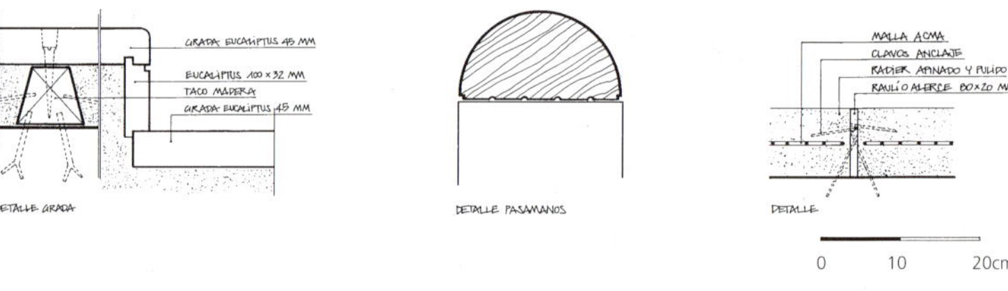

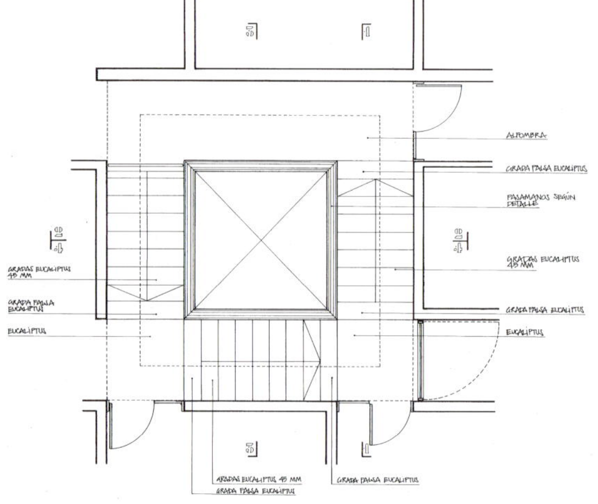

Main Staircase Section, Details and Plan

Errazuriz House

Villarrica, Chile

Located on the north bank of Lake Villarrica, 435 miles (700 kilometers) south of Santiago, this house lies on a property of about 247 acres (100 hectares), densely covered with native trees. From it there is a breathtaking view of the Villarrica volcano, located south of the lake. The site is relatively plain as far as the edge of the lake, where it falls sharply some fifty-nine feet (eighteen meters) down to the beach level and the water.

The challenge posed by this house was developing a project that architecturally links the upper plane of the property with the plane of the beach and the lake. The project also needed to safeguard the woods covering the site, the cliff, and the beach edge. A radical stance was taken, consisting of building the house on the stretch of ground between the cliff wall and the beach. Its upper terrace would be built at the woods level, without obstructing the view toward the lake and the volcano. The house itself becomes the element functionally and architecturally relating both planes.

The house, with its three stories and terraces, leans on huge buttresses of exposed concrete, and its capricious planimetry is a rigorous adaptation to the trees existing in the place. The house is entirely made of reinforced exposed concrete, both on the inside and the outside.

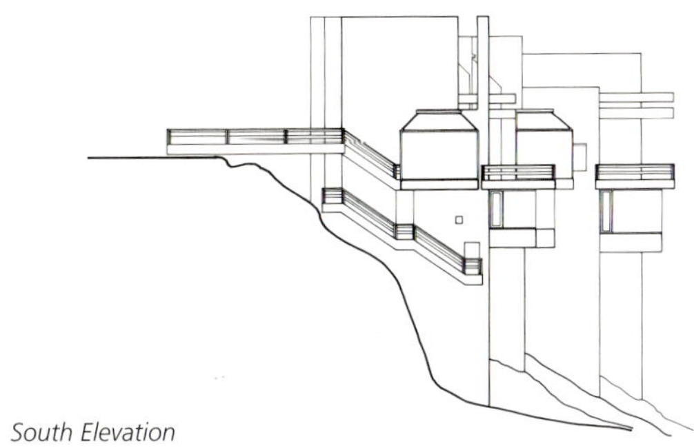

South Elevation

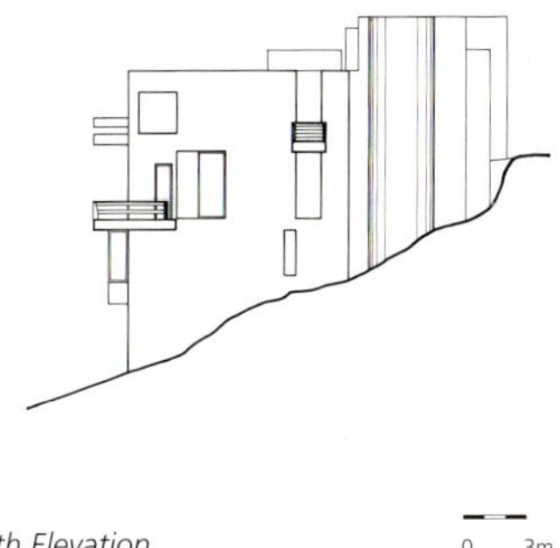

North Elevation

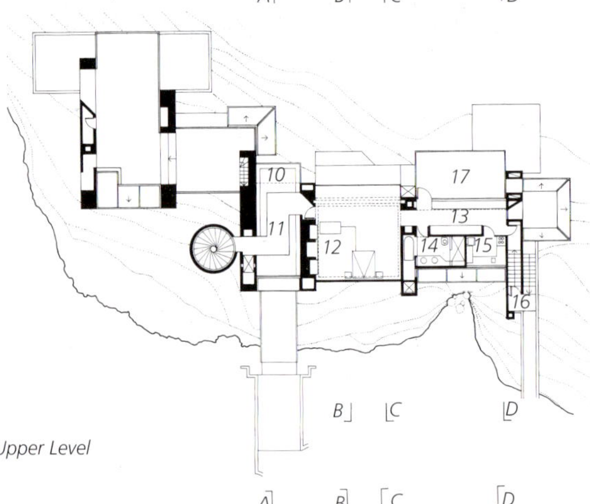

Upper Level

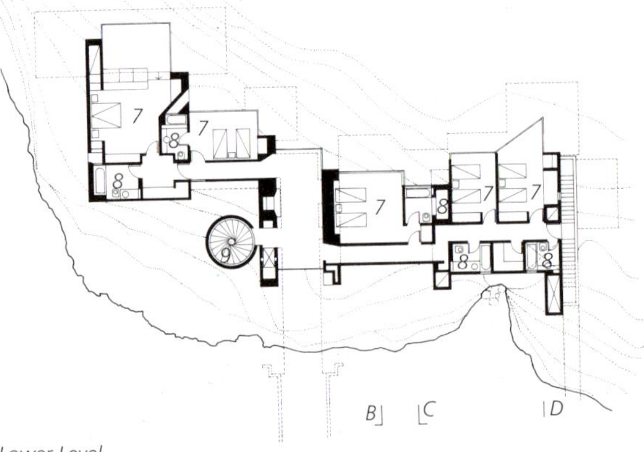

Lower Level

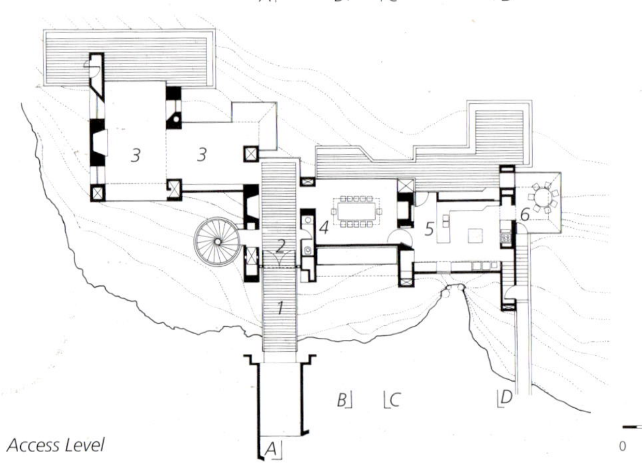

Access Level

0 3m

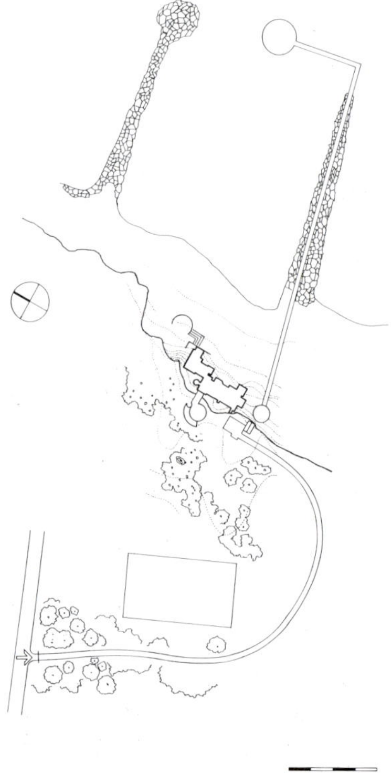
Site Plan

0 40m

1. Bridge
2. Entrance Hall
3. Living Room
4. Dining Room
5. Kitchen
6. Service Dining Room
7. Bedrooms
8. Bathrooms
9. Staircase
10. Gallery
11. Bridge
12. Master Bedroom
13. Walk-in Closet
14. Bathroom
15. Kitchenette
16. Second Entrance
17. Terrace

This Page: Upper photograph: the lake has a protected area for the anchoring of different sorts of pleasure boats delimited by two rocky breakwaters. Lower photographs: roofed area among the trees used as carport and as a rain-protected access to the house.

Opposite Page: Upper photograph: approach from the lake. Lower photograph: boathouse with upper lookout terrace.

This Page: *Beautiful concentric grooves embellish the modest concrete pavement of the circular access patio of this house.*

Opposite Page: *The circular access patio and the bridge leading to the front door.*

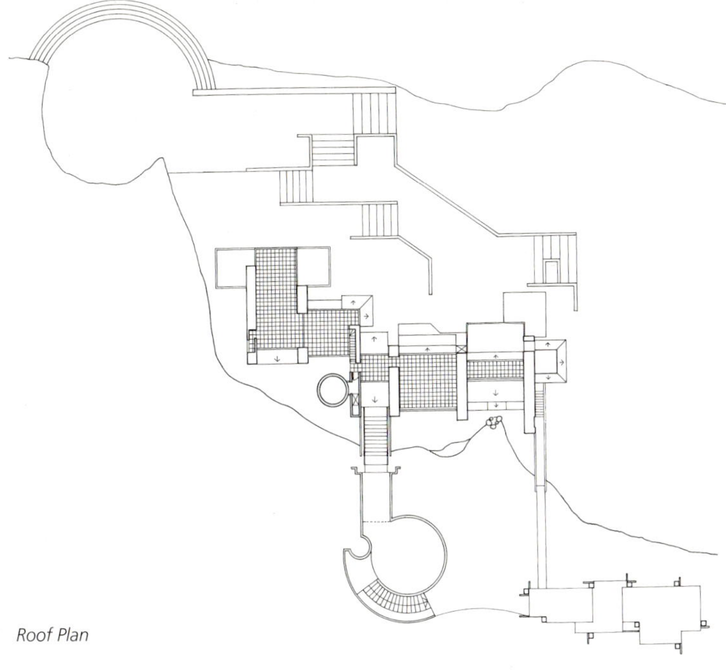

Roof Plan

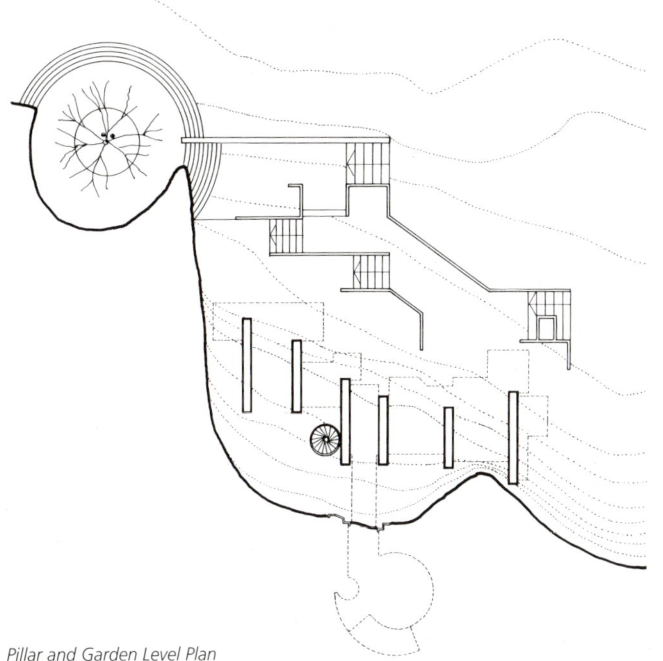

Pillar and Garden Level Plan

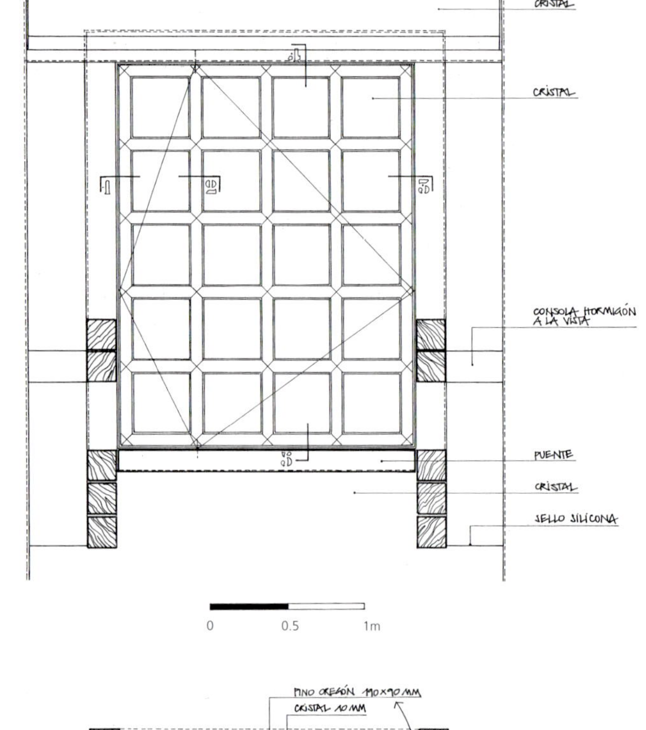

This Page: *Detail of the access bridge and of the triple-height main hall, crossed by a wooden deck leading to the master bedroom.*

Opposite Page: *The triple-height main access hall, showing the treatment of the exposed concrete of one of the buttresses, which includes a small chimney.*

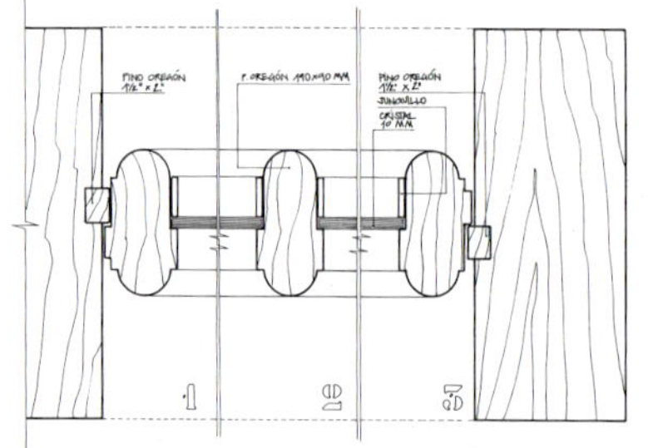

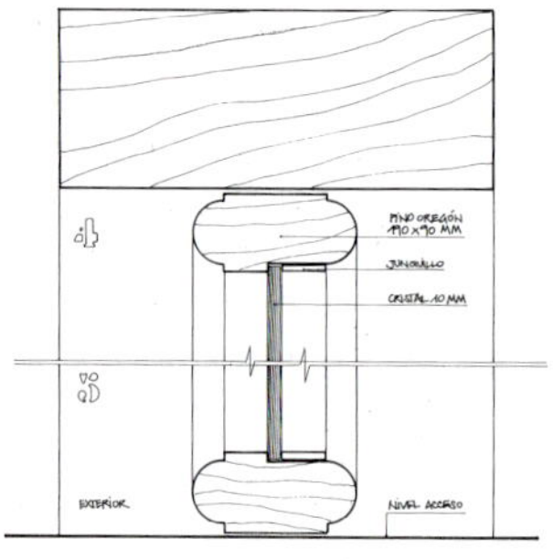

Main Access Door Section, Plan, and Details

0   10   20cm

This Page: The spiral staircase connecting the different levels. Its steps are of solid oak, adze-worked in situ. The steps detach from the wall to allow the entrance of light from the upper skylight.

Opposite Page: The ceiling of the staircase forms a continuous helicoidal plane.

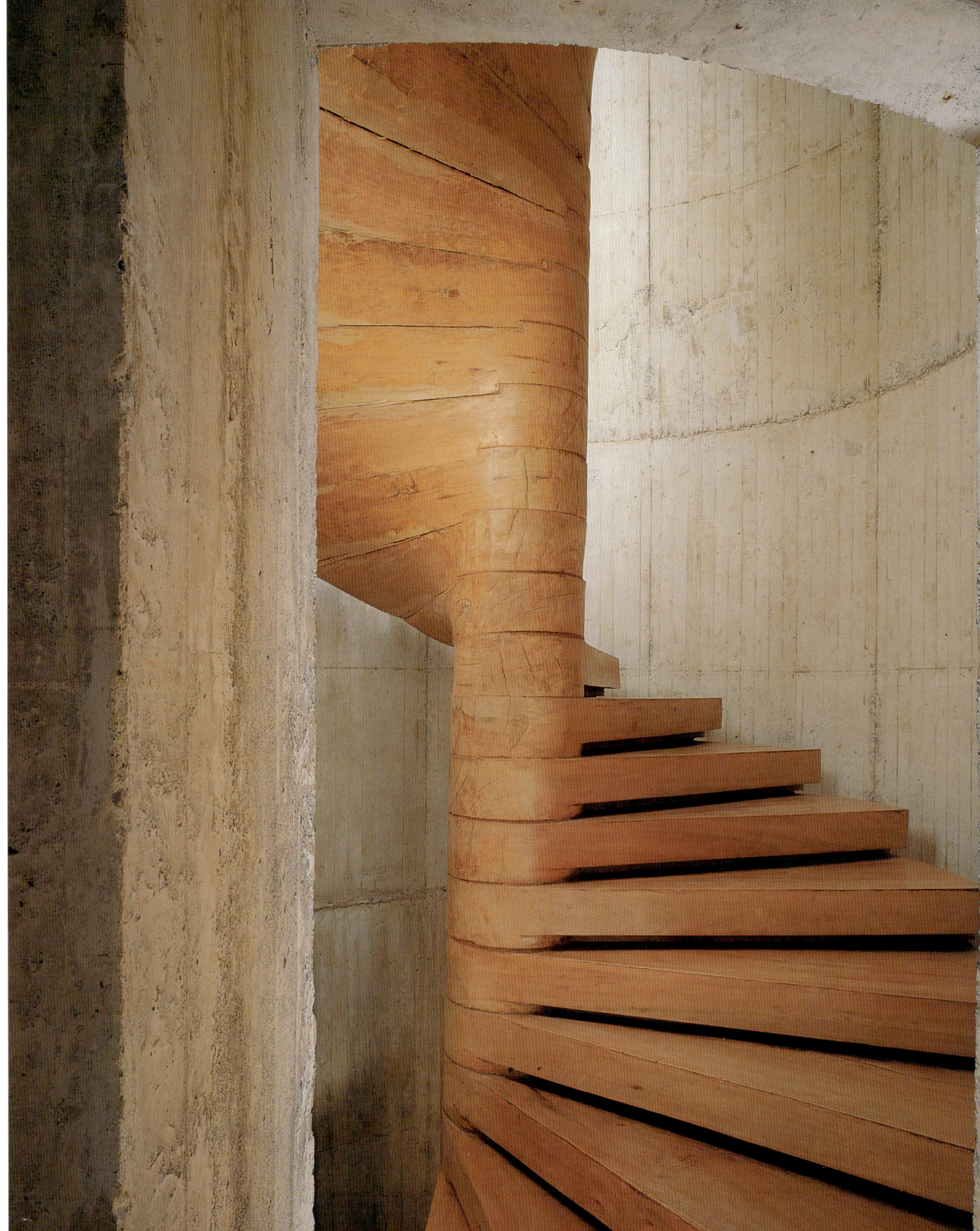

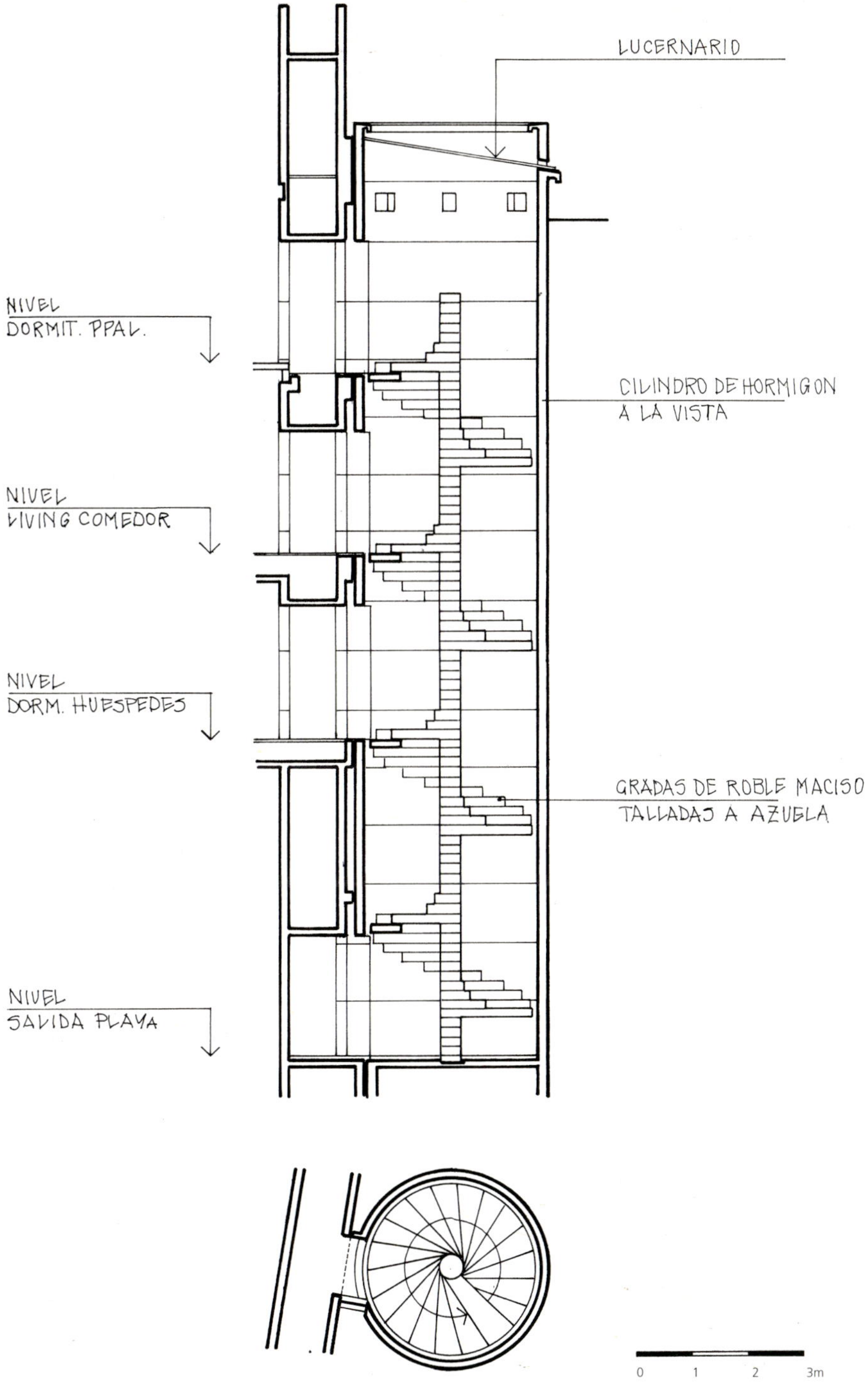

Helicoidal Stair Detail

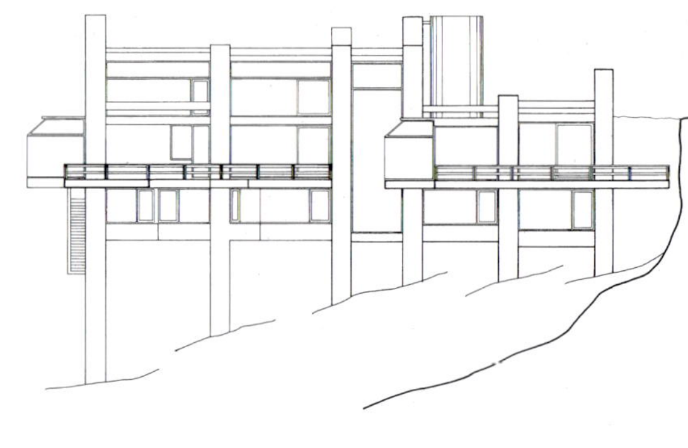

East Elevation

0   3m

Axonometric View

This Page: *The buttresses are hollow and contain stairs, an elevator, a guest bathroom, equipment, chimneys, etc.*

Opposite Page: *The gap in one of the buttresses connecting the access hall with the living room exposes the dinning room at the back.*

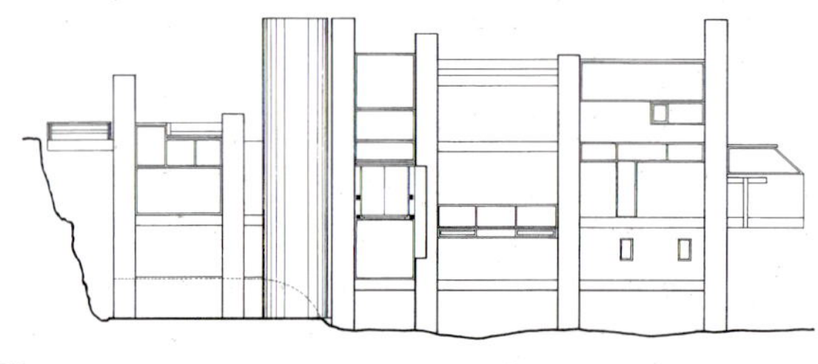

West Elevation

0   3m

Section C-C

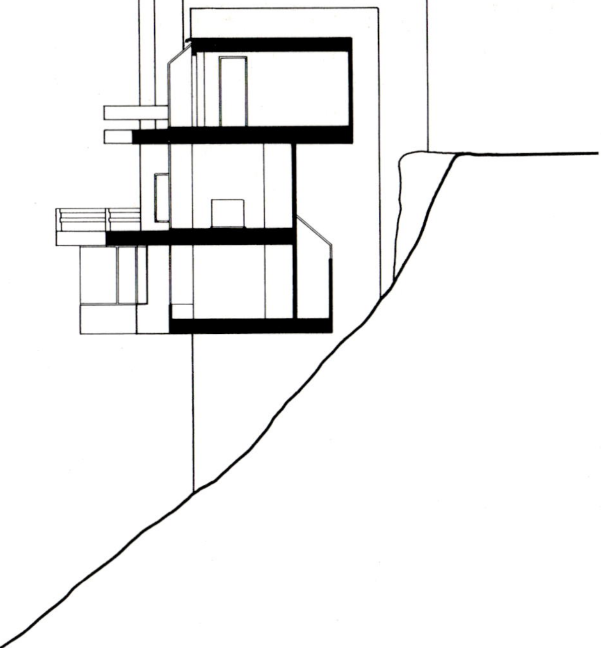

Section D-D

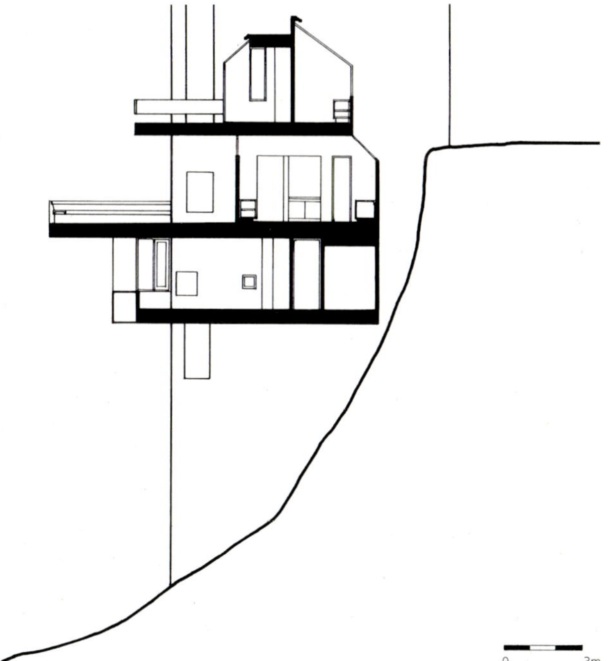

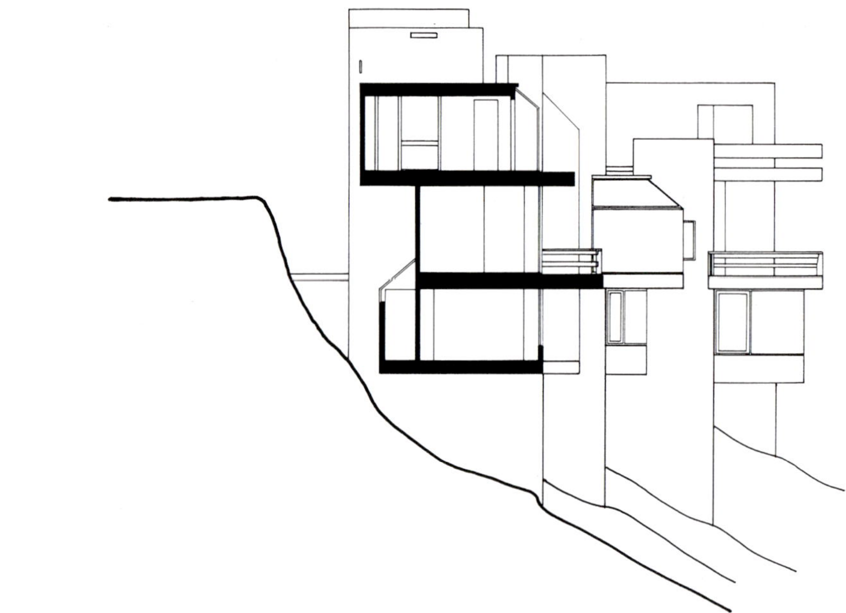

Section B-B

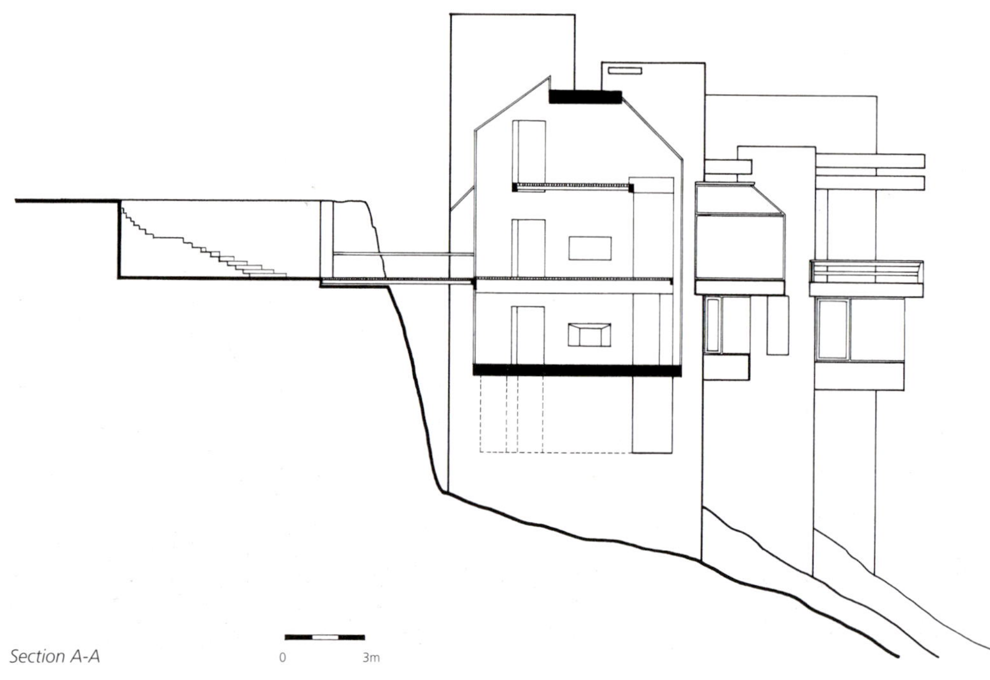

Section A-A

0   3m

The "El Condor" Group

Santiago, Chile

To develop these three houses, a series of goals was established: to produce a strong group relationship; to create a geography adapted to the characteristics of the place and its vegetation—palm trees, conifers, thorny acacias, and poplars; and to concentrate on the relation of the houses to the large private park belonging to the former owners of the entire sector. The group relationship rests mainly on the incorporation of a cylinder as a recognizable common form and on a system of terraces stretching over the three sites that unifies the base of the cylinders.

The use of the terrace roof as a noble and fundamental feature of the house becomes particularly valuable in the Chilean climate and geography. The appearance of a "dual layer," a real architecture inside another, is formed by the cylinder that circumscribes an orthogonal architecture which sometimes approaches it, as others detach from or become incorporated with it, creating a series of intermediate spaces between the exterior and the interior.

The cylinder acts as a sort of "spatial hinge" that dominates the surrounding space, branching out in all directions. The role of this spatial hinge kept changing, from the first house built, the Fajnzylbers', until ending in the impressive volume of our own house, which makes the street look as if traced after its construction. The substance of the work, speaking of the three houses as a whole, was defined by giving a different treatment to each cylinder, leaning them on terraces with retaining walls of exposed concrete that grant them unity. Likewise, the stone of the cylinder of the Chadwick House is repeated in the retaining wall surrounding our house. Given the prevailing south and southwest exposure of the three sites, the cylinder also reflects the light coming from the north toward the interior of the houses. That is why in the El Condor House, the upper skylight plays the role of a window open to the sun in 360 degrees.

There is also a formal resonance with the upward limit imposed on the site by the El Condor street; still more important is the counterpoint of the cylinder with the inner orthogonal system and its capability to create such introverted and intimate spaces, to produce a surprising world of intermediate places between the exterior and the interior.

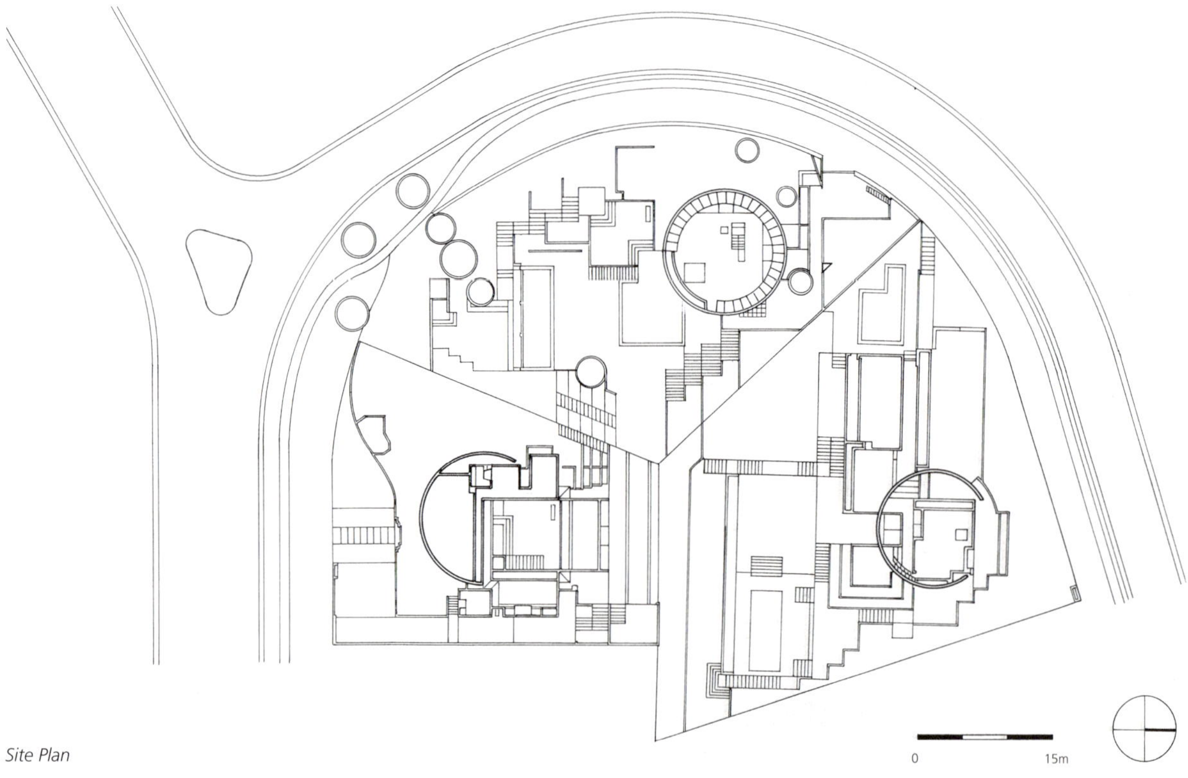

Site Plan

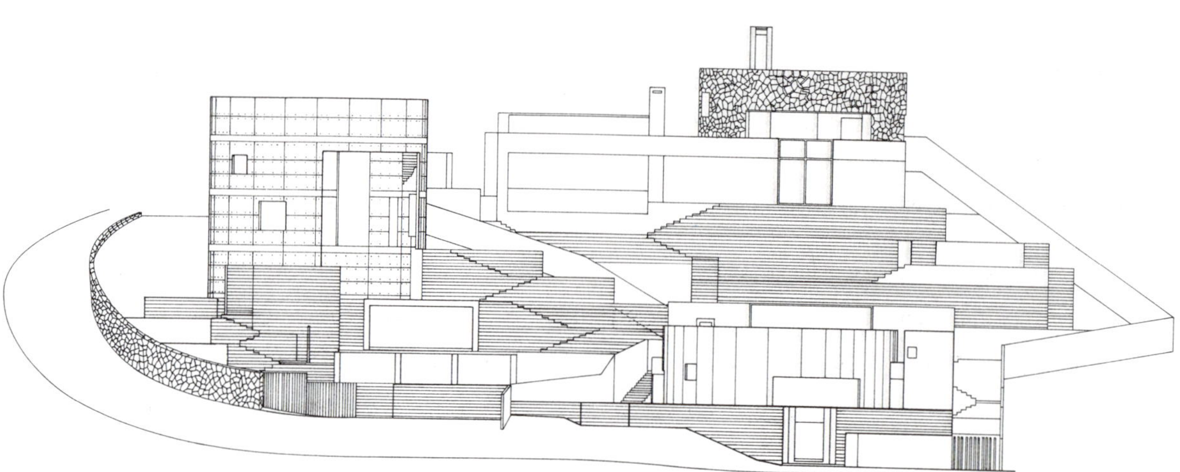

Group Elevation

In these houses—due to requirements of the first two clients themselves and coincidental with a search present in our last works—the need appeared not only to subordinate the window to the cylinders' planes, but to literally eliminate it. Thus, the three houses have several and very particular ways of relating with the outside. The interior of the houses is also stressed by their peculiar accesses: a tunnel in the Fajnzylber House, and a walled patio in the Chadwick House.

In the El Condor House, a succession of spatial situations consists of patios, stairs, turns, etc., which, on reaching the true access, have the visitor submerged in a world totally different to the outside one. In one of these turns, especially from the upper patio, the Rabat Park appears with a strength and richness not fully appreciated from outside. That is to say that in the three cases, and thanks to different resources, the outside world has disappeared before entering the houses.

This Spread: A continuous system of terraces and contention walls going through the three sites makes it possible to negotiate the great difference existing between the three cylinders.

Opposite Page: The three houses' ground plan and elevation account for the unitary treatment of the group, in which the three cylinders stand out for their height and materiality.

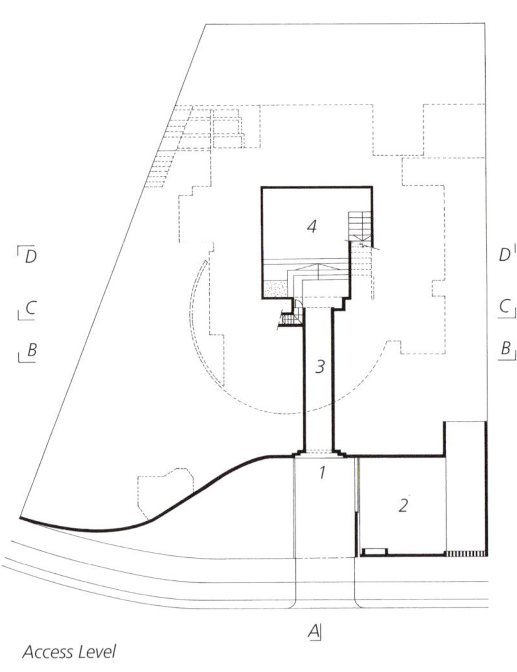

Access Level

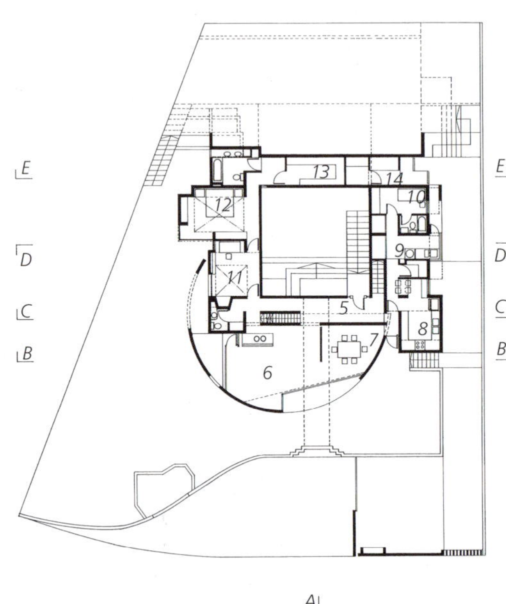

Main Floor Plan

Upper Floor Plan

Fajnzylber House

1. Entrance
2. Carport
3. Tunnel
4. Patio
5. Entrance Hall
6. Living Room
7. Dining Room
8. Kitchen
9. Laundry
10. Service Bedroom
11. Studio
12. Master Bedroom
13. Walk-in Closet
14. Mechanical
15. Children's Bedroom
16. Upper Studio
17. Terrace

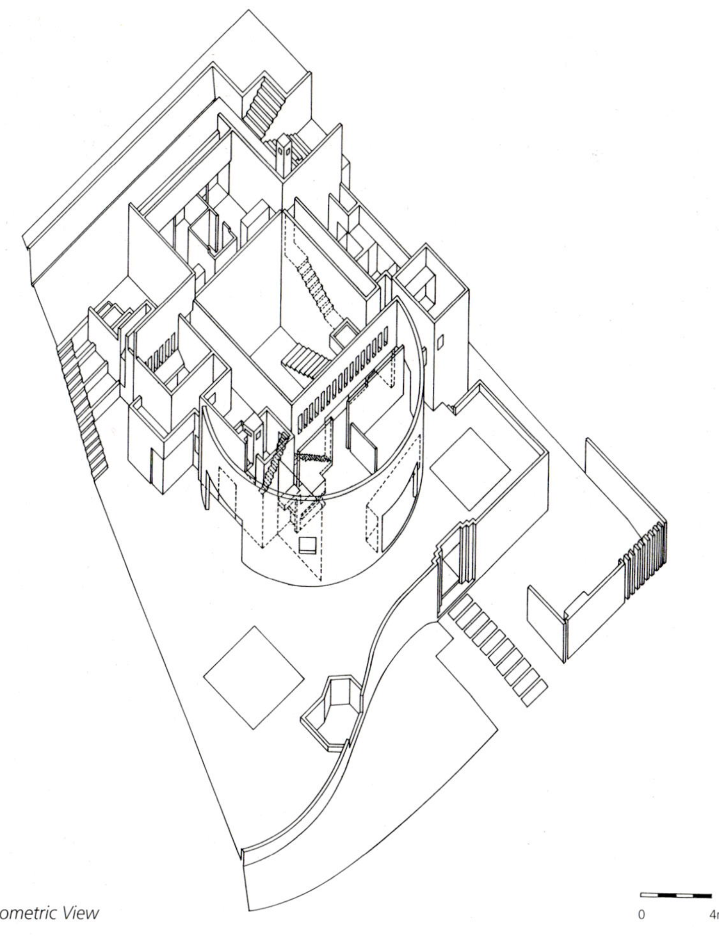

Axonometric View

0   4m

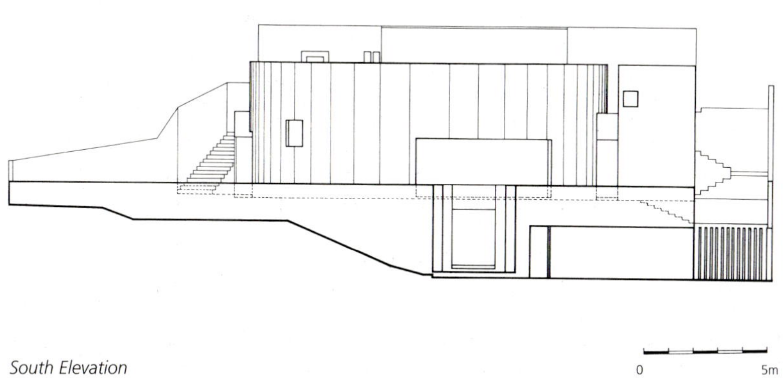

South Elevation

0   5m

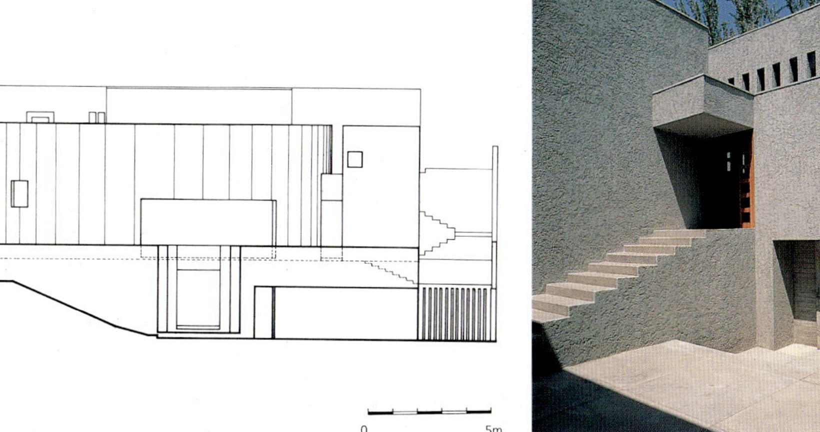

This Page: *The Fajnzylber House, the most stern of the three, with walls of reinforced masonry, coarse stucco, and floors of polished concrete.*

Opposite Page: *The patio, an eight meter cube of polished concrete floor, is accessed through a tunnel.*

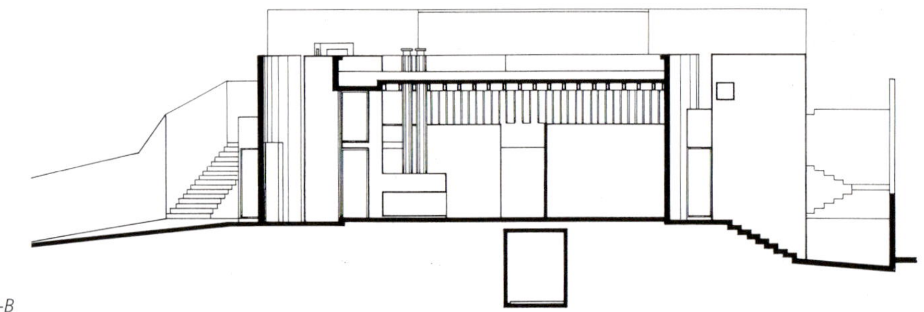

Section B-B

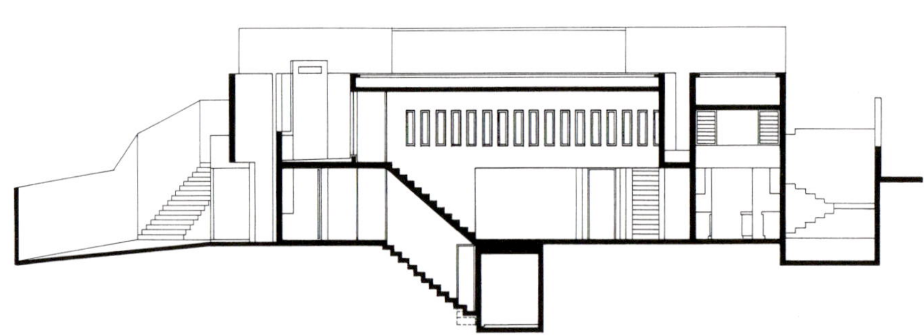

Section C-C

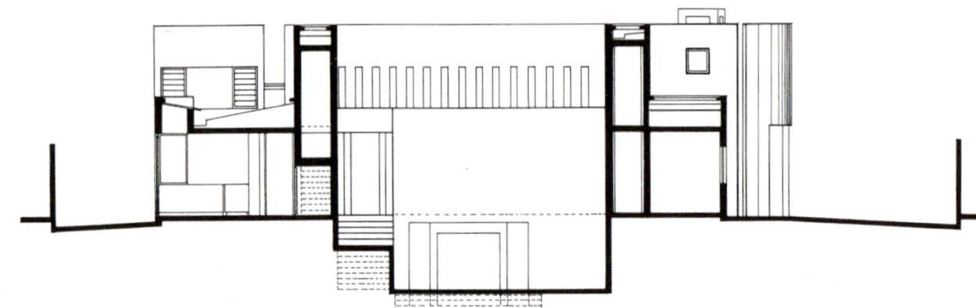

Section D-D

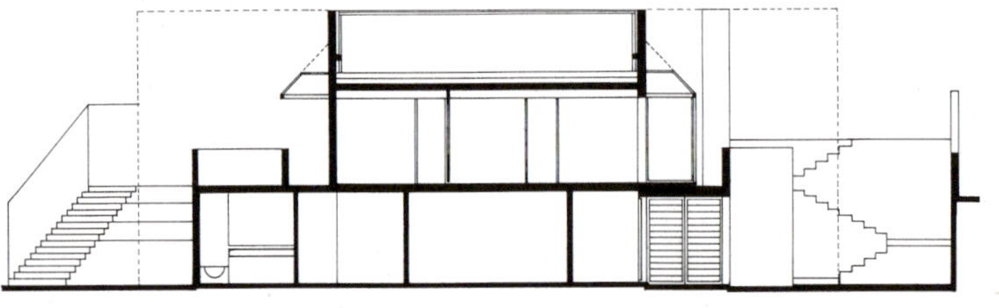

Section E-E

This Page: *The sternness of materials throughout the house is compensated by the spatial richness and the unexpected dimensions.*

Opposite Page: *Concrete furniture, specially designed for this house, occupies a shady spot of the garden.*

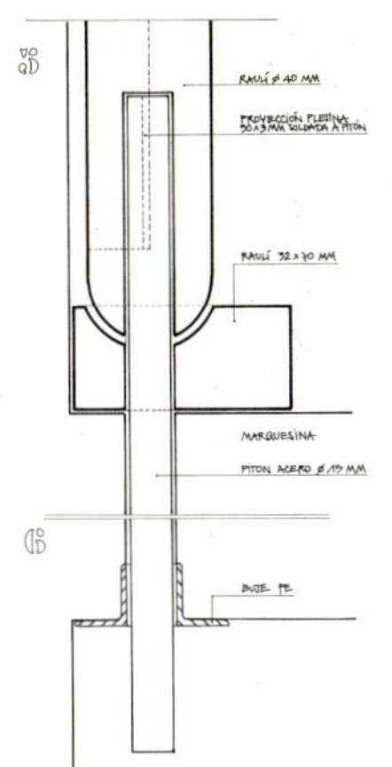
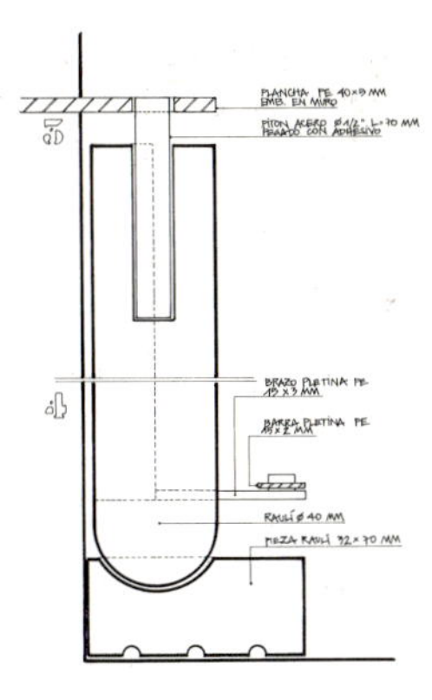
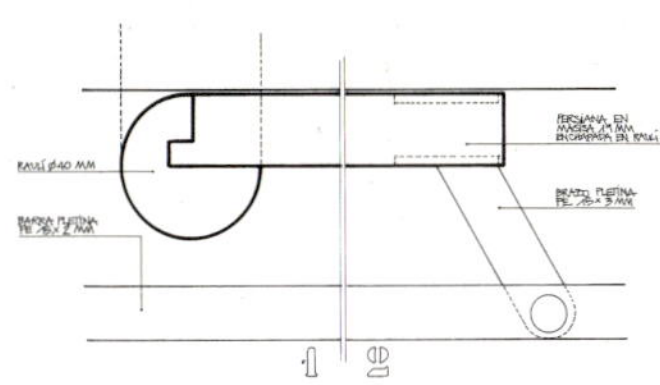
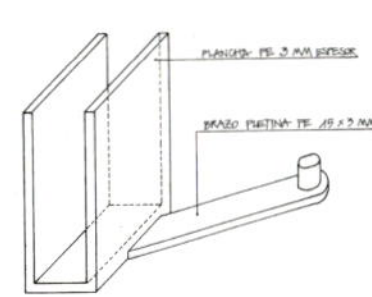
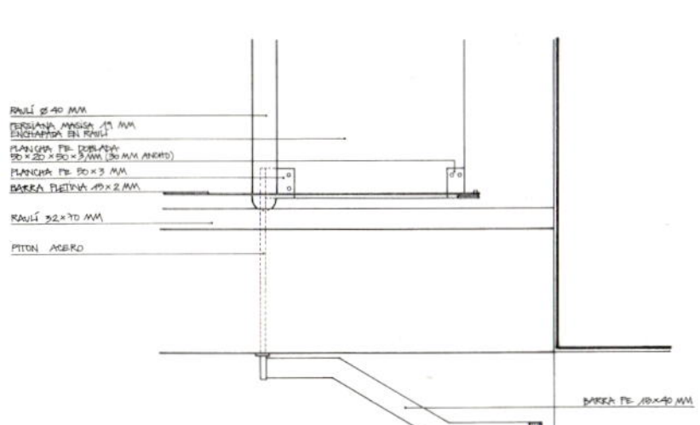

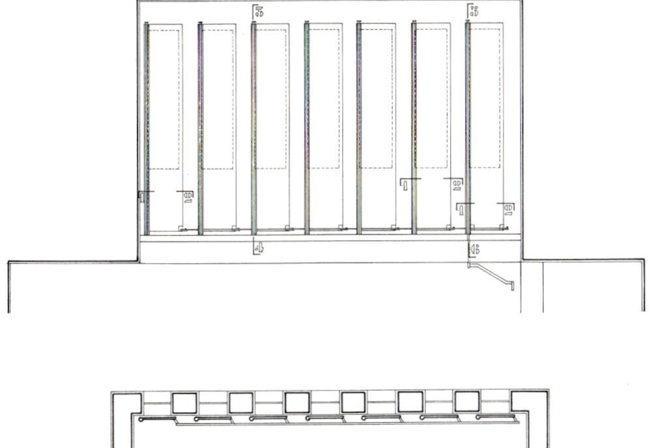
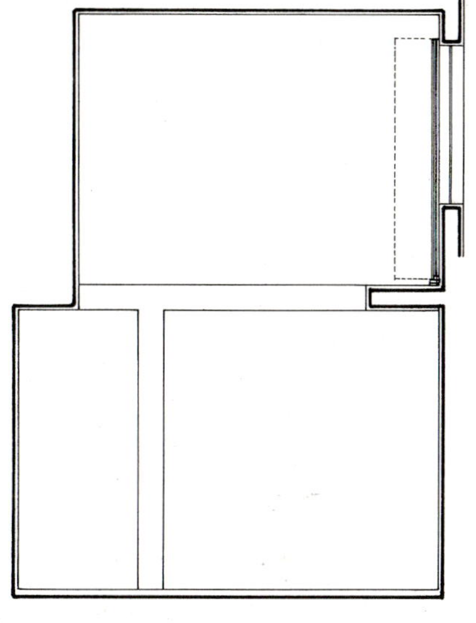

Master Bedroom Blind Elevation, Plan, Section, and Details

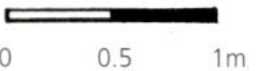

Third Floor Plan

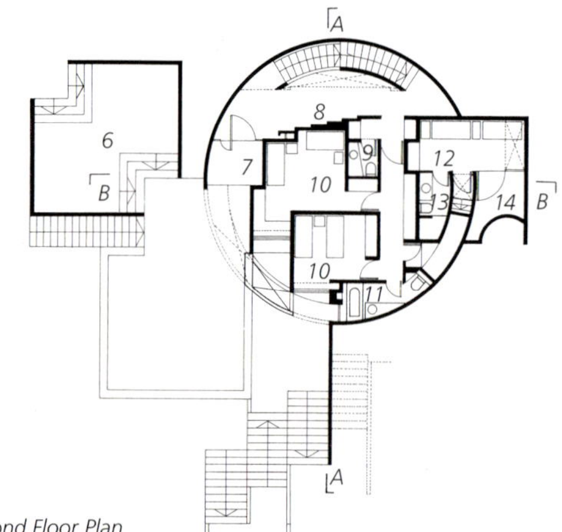

El Condor House

1. Terrace
2. Studio
3. Powder Room
4. Library
5. Ramp
6. Patio
7. Main Entrance
8. Hall
9. Guest Bathroom
10. Bedroom
11. Bathroom
12. Service Room
13. Service Bathroom
14. Service Patio
15. Secondary Entrance
16. Living Room
17. Dining Room
18. Kitchen
19. Laundry
20. Master Bedroom
21. Master Bathroom
22. Roof Terrace

Second Floor Plan

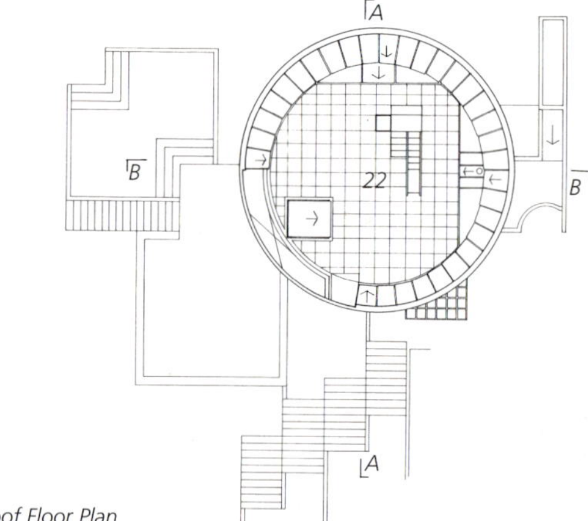

Roof Floor Plan

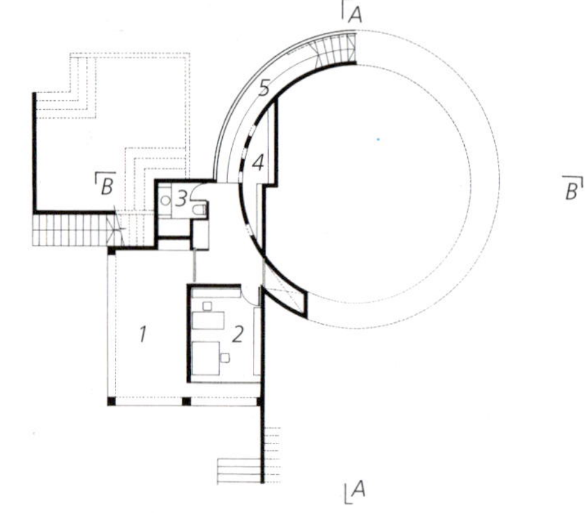

First Floor Plan

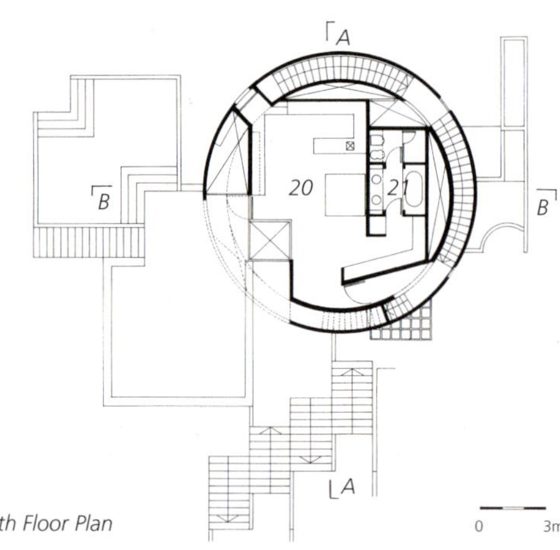

Fourth Floor Plan

0   3m

Previous Spread: *The turret of the architect's house stands out as the dominant cylinder of the group.*

This Page: *The climbing plant in the upper photograph has been thought to act as a natural thermic protection against the cylinder's western exposure.*

Opposite Page: *The axonometric view shows the system of terraces and stairs thoroughly covering the site and acting as the turret's base.*

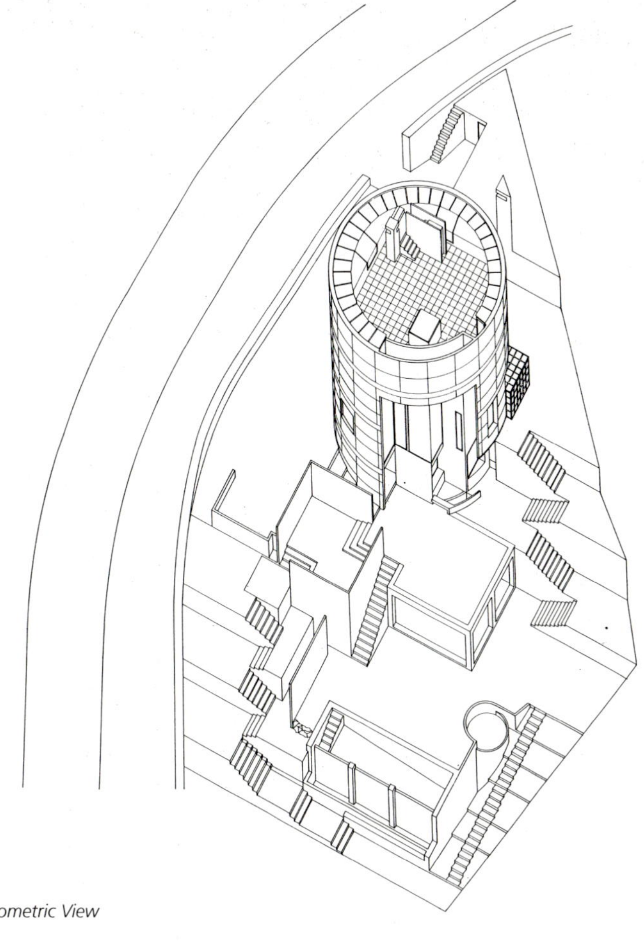

Axonometric View

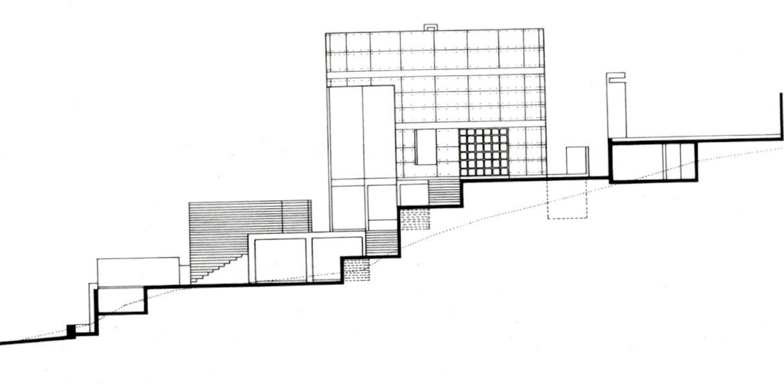

East Section/Elevation

0 ___ 4m

This Page: The large circular boring of the inner cylinder visually enlarges the size of the access hall.

Opposite Page: The staircase detaches from the outer cylinder so as not to interrupt the continuity of the wall and to allow the natural lighting of the flight of stairs leading to the studio. The concrete molding is of plywood and it was given a single use.

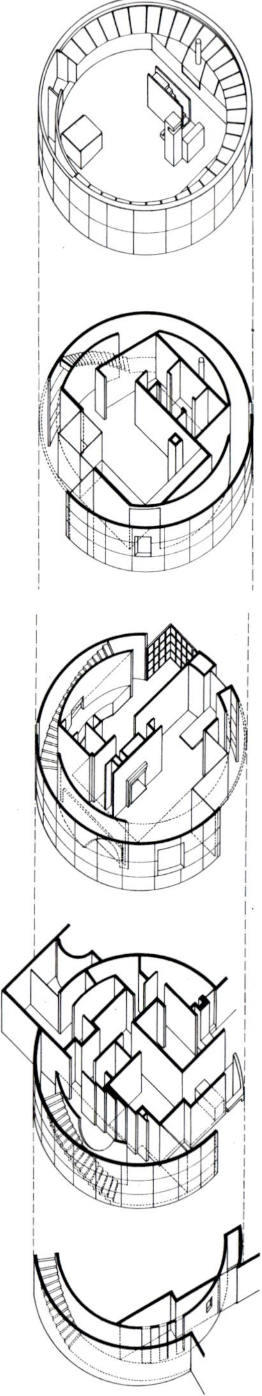

Exploded Axonometric View

0   5m

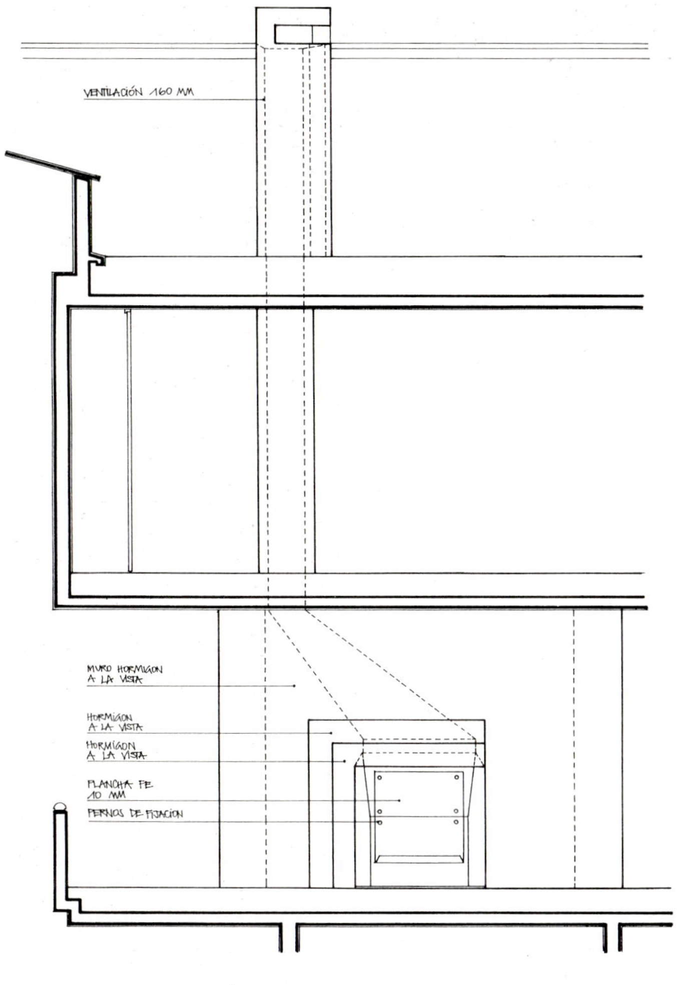

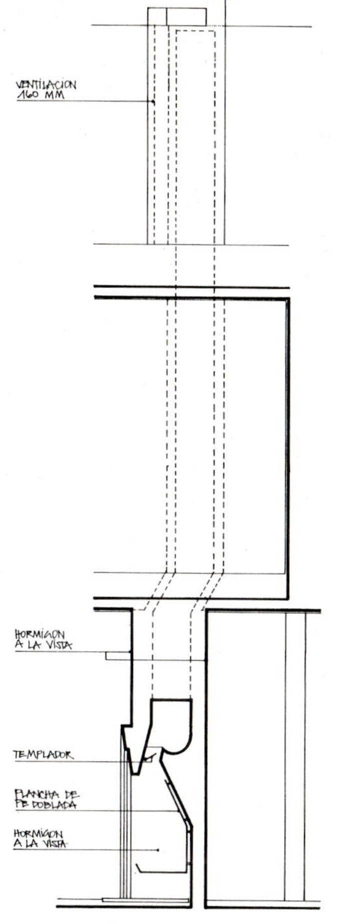

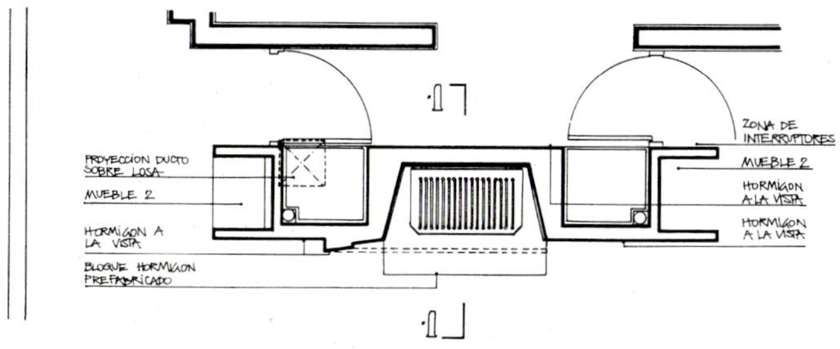

Fireplace Plan, Elevation, and Section

0   1m

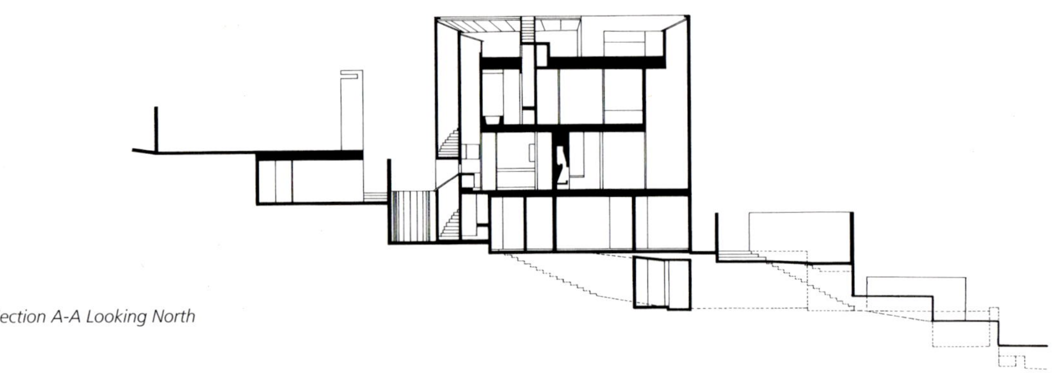

Section A-A Looking North

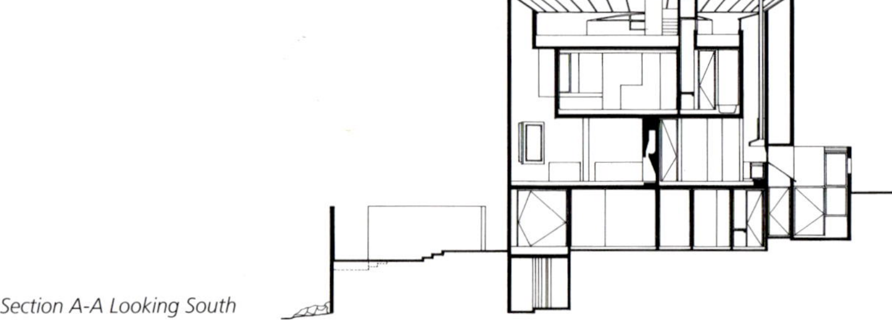

Section A-A Looking South

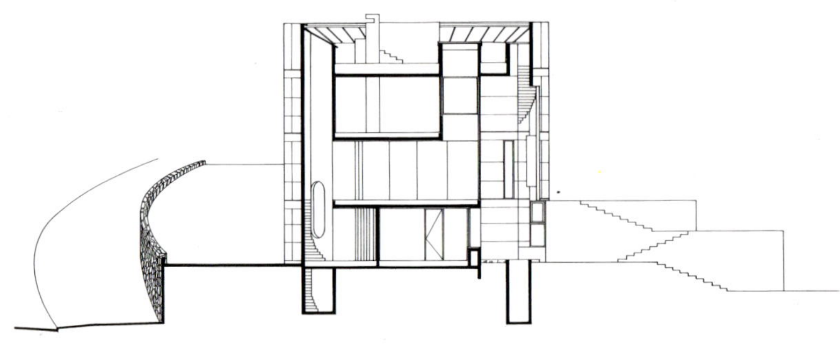

Section

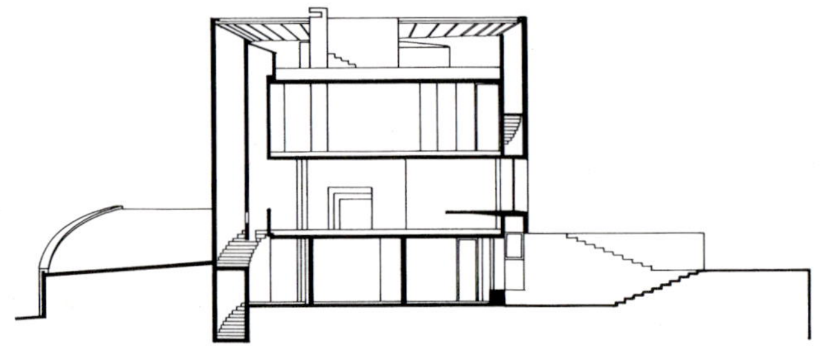

Section B-B

This Page: *The upper photograph shows the master bedroom, a wooden orthogonal box inserted in the cylinder.*

Opposite Page: *Details of the living room and dining room area, revealing the delicate control of the cylinder's perforations which direct the view toward the park of the neighboring estate.*

This Page: *The Chadwick House, located at the top of the site, shows a cylinder lined with a richly textured stone and covered with moss.*

Opposite Page: *Lower photograph: The stoutly terraced garden follows the profile of the hills behind the house.*

Chadwick House

1. Access
2. Carport
3. Enclosed Garden
4. Entry
5. Living Room
6. Dining Room
7. Kitchen
8. Service Bedroom
9. Service Bathroom
10. Laundry
11. Study
12. Bedroom
13. Swimming Pool
14. Master Bedroom

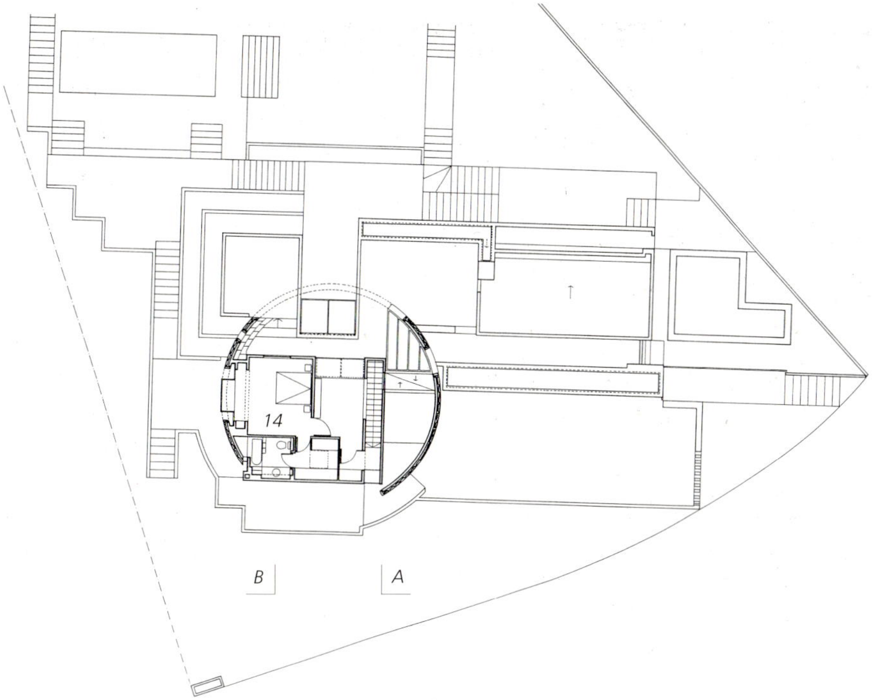

Upper Floor Plan

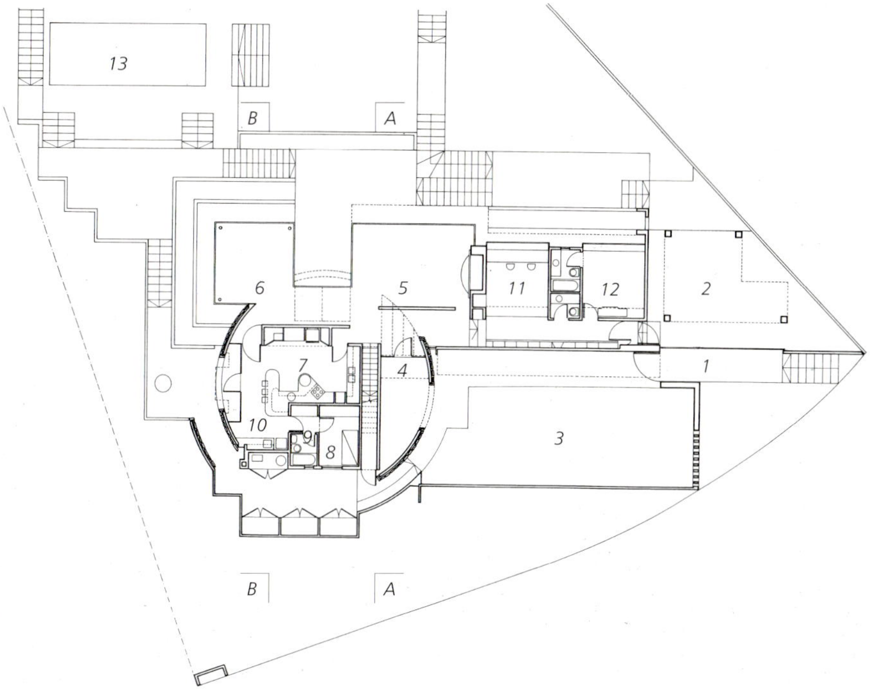

Lower Floor Plan

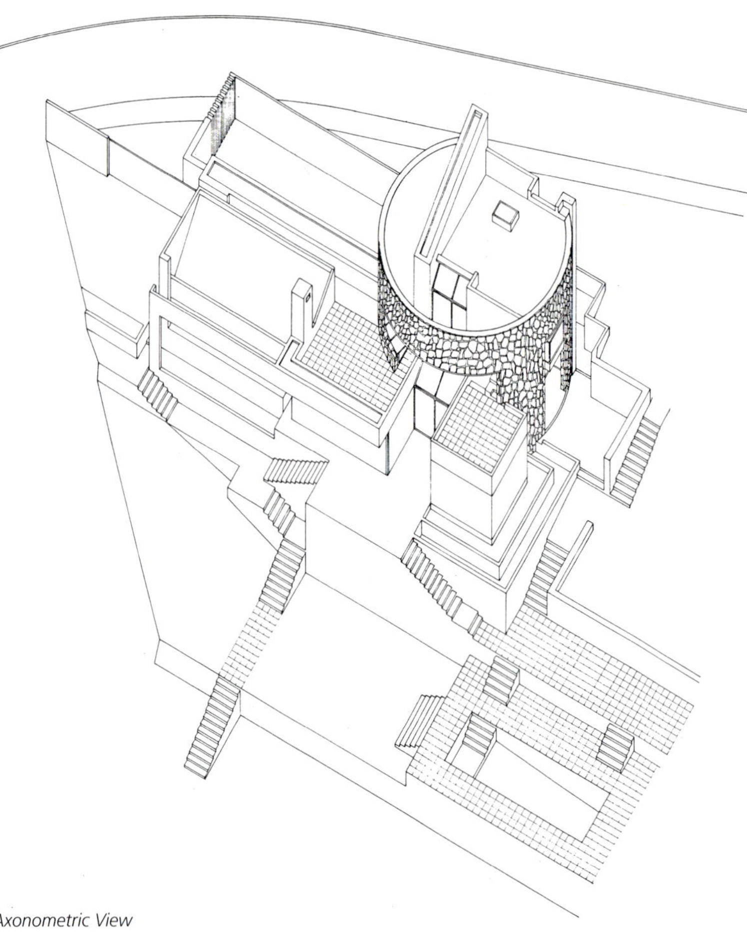

Axonometric View

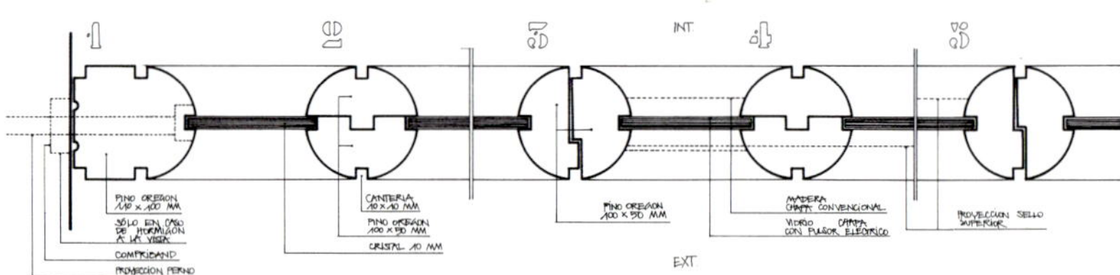

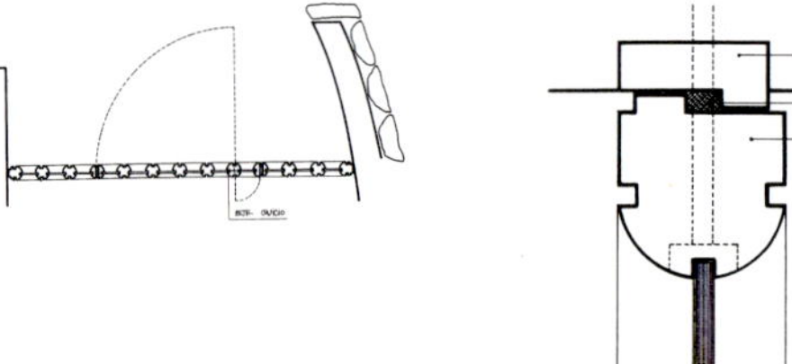

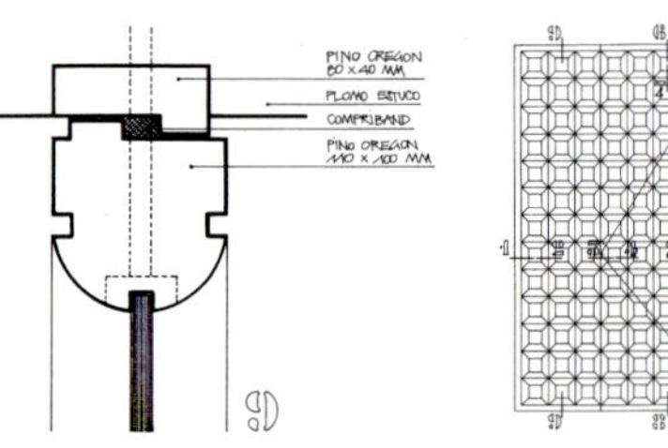

Access Door Plan and Details

This Page and Opposite: *The front door, lavishly worked in Oregon pine and glass, contrasts with the magnitude of the outer access space, and constitutes a big wedge between the cylinder and a wall belonging to the orthogonal system of the house.*

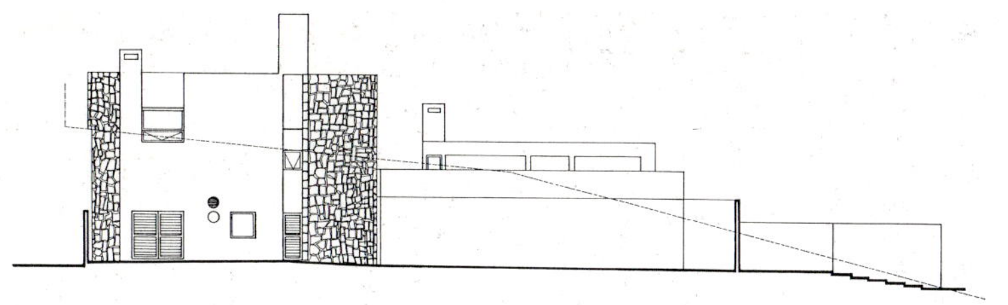

North Elevation

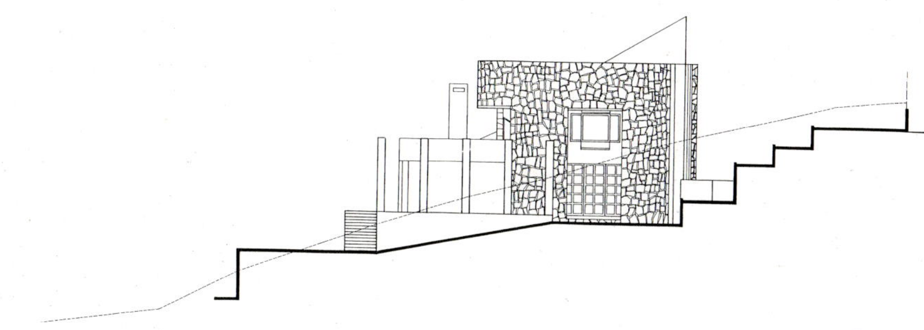

East Elevation

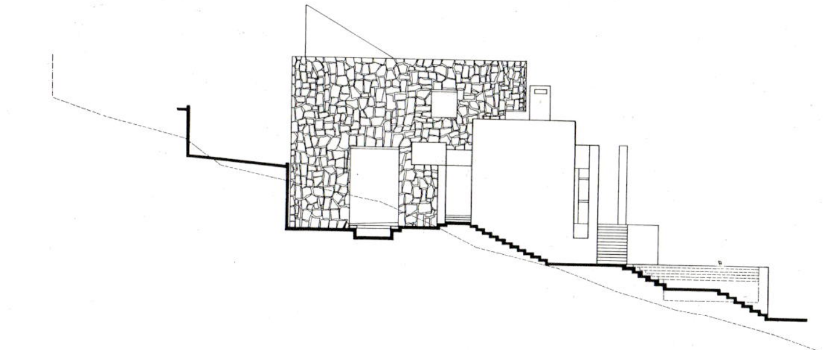

West Elevation

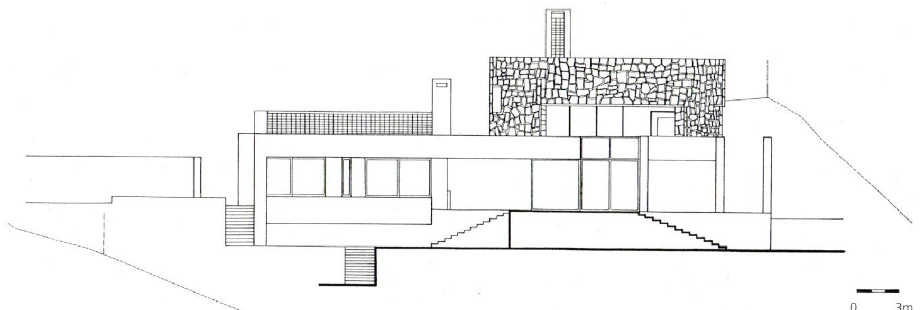

South Elevation

Selected Buildings and Projects

Garcia House
Santiago, Chile
Architect: Christian de Groote
Associate Architect: Hugo Molina
Structural Engineering: Luis Soler &
Associates
Site: 33,600 sf (3,125 sm)
Building: 6,030 sf (560 sm)
Date of Design: 1981
Construction Completion: 1982

Constanza Vergara House
Algarrobo, Chile
Architect: Christian de Groote
Associate Architect: Hugo Molina
Structural Engineering: Luis Soler &
Associates
Site: 4,736 sf (440 sm)
Building: 2,700 sf (250 sm)
Date of Design: 1980
Construction Completion: 1981

Fuenzalida House
Santiago, Chile
Architect: Christian de Groote
Associate Architect: Hugo Molina
Structural Engineering: Fernando
del Sol/Hartmut Vogel
Site: 27,000 sf (2,500 sm)
Building: 4,500 sf (420 sm)
Date of Design: 1982
Construction Completion: 1983

Gellona House
Santiago, Chile
Architects: Christian de Groote
Associated Architect: Hugo Molina
Structural Engineering: Larrain, Ruiz,
Saavedra
Site: 270,000 sf (25,220 sm)
Building: 11,250 sf (1,045 sm)
Date of Design: 1983
Construction Completion: 1985

Matte House
Zapallar, Chile
Architect: Christian de Groote
Associate Architect: Hugo Molina
Structural Engineering: Luis Soler &
Associates
Site: 54,250 sf (5,040 sm)
Building: 4,725 sf (439 sm)
Date of Design: 1986
Construction Completion: 1987

Orrego House
El Pangue, Chile
Architect: Christian de Groote
Associate Architect: Hugo Molina
Structural Engineering: Luis Soler &
Associates
Site: 95,000 sf (8,829 sm)
Building: 3,850 sf (357 sm)
Date of Design: 1988
Construction Completion: 1989

Elisa House
Santiago, Chile
Architect: Christian de Groote
Associate Architect: Camila del Fierro
Structural Engineering: Luis Soler &
Associates
Site: 64,600 sf (6,000 sm)
Building: 10,400 sf (967 sm)
Date of Design: 1988
Construction Completion: 1990

La Cumbre House
Santiago, Chile
Architects: Christian de Groote,
Camila del Fierro
Structural Engineering: Jorge Barthou
Site: 12,500 sf (1,159 sm)
Building: 3,400 sf (315 sm)
Date of Design: 1991
Construction Completion: 1993

Errazuriz House
Villarrica, Chile
Architect: Christian de Groote
Associate Architect: Berta Errazuriz
Structural Engineering: Luis Soler &
Associates
Site: 247 a (100 ha)
Building: 6,000 sf (550 sm)
Date of Design: 1991
Construction Completion: 1993

The "El Condor" Group
Fajnzylber House
Santiago, Chile
Architects: Christian de Groote,
Camila del Fierro
Structural Engineering: Luis Soler & Assoc.
Site: 10,800 sf (1,000 sm)
Building: 2,800 sf (259 sm)
Date of Design: 1987
Construction Completion: 1989

El Condor House
Santiago, Chile
Architects: Christian de Groote,
Camila del Fierro
Structural Engineering: Luis Soler &
Associates
Site: 15,070 sf (1,400 sm)
Building: 4,850 sf (450 sm)
Date of Design: 1988
Construction Completion: 1993–1995

Chadwick House
Santiago, Chile
Architects: Christian de Groote
Associate Architect: Camila del Fierro
Structural Engineering: Luis Soler &
Associates
Site: 18,100 sf (1,685 sm)
Building: 2,900 sf (267 sm)
Date of Design: 1988
Construction Completion: 1989

Firm Profile

The firm Christian de Groote Associated Architects was founded in 1967, on ending de Groote's former association with architect Emilio Duhart. Starting from that time, de Groote has had several associated architects, standing out among them Hugo Molina, who left the office at the end of 1996. The composition of the firm has ranged from eight employees to the present twenty-six; its current associated architect is Camila del Fierro, married to Christian de Groote.

Christian de Groote, born in Chile in 1931, lived part of his youth in Cuba, and part in Mexico, where he graduated from high school. He studied Architecture at the Pontificia Universidad Católica de Chile (the country's most reputed Catholic university) where he took his degree in 1958 with the highest grade. Later on, he obtained a scholarship from the Fulbright Foundation and the U.S. State Department, taking postgraduate studies at M.I.T., in Chicago, and at the University of California in Berkeley.

On his return to Chile in 1961, he worked for the firm of Emilio Duhart—the most reputed architect of the time—where, as associated architect, de Groote participated in the competition for the United Nations building in Santiago; the firm took first prize. Starting on 1967, de Groote established his own office, designing many works for industrial and mining concerns, offices, newspapers, and banks, creating buildings, malls, exhibition pavilions, social housing, graphic design. Yet a very important proportion of his work has been devoted to private houses, de Groote having built more than 150 houses to date.

Paralleling his professional activities, de Groote has participated in many competitions, both domestic and international, the most important being the competitions for the Teheran Library; for the Tête Defense Building in Paris; and for the remodeling of the Prado Museum in Madrid. His works have won awards in different biennial architecture exhibitions held in Santiago and have been published in many books and magazines, both domestic and foreign.

Christian de Groote has been, at different times, a visiting professor on the Faculty of Architecture of the Pontificia Universidad Católica de Chile, in Santiago. In 1993, that university's architecture faculty published a monograph of his work titled *The Architecture of Three Decades of Work* (ARQ Publications). The same year, he won the National Architecture Award, Chile's top prize. In December 1997, he won the Vitrubio Award, granted by the Museum of Fine Arts, Buenos Aires, Argentina.

Photographic Credits